A Life Planning Guide for Women

Mary Vander Goot

A Life Planning Guide for Women

PAIDEIA PRESS
Jordan Station, Ontario, Canada

THE EDWIN MELLEN PRESS
New York

HQ
1206
.V3
1982

Cover quilt designed and pieced by Nancy Crow. Hand-quilting by Mrs. Levi Mast. Titled: *November I,* © **1980, Baltimore, Ohio. 64" x 64". Photograph courtesy of the artist.**

ISBN 0-88815-074-1

Published simultaneously in the United States by The Edwin Mellen Press, Box 450, Lewiston, New York 14092 (716-754-8566).

ISBN 0-88946-512-6
Printed in Canada.

Contents

Preface

Every book has a starting point, and every author a point of view. Most books about women are feminist or traditional, and if this book were either traditional or feminist, I would let the reader guess my position. I do not defend either of these positions, however, because I believe there is a more hopeful starting point which can be found in the essence of the Christian faith.

The message of the Christian faith is one of freedom, the key to which is this: we are to make actual in our lives the belief that the only absolute loyalty, the only ultimate commitment, the only sure authority, is God. The person who is grounded in this loyalty is one who:

> . . . lives in faith, who has given over the meaning of life to his [her] Creator, and who lives centered on the energies of his [her] Maker . . . He [she] is fully in the world on its terms and wholly beyond the world in his [her] trust of the invisible dimension . . . The great strength of such an ideal is that it allows one to be open, generous, courageous, to touch others' lives and enrich them and open them in turn.[1]

Absolute reliance on God is displayed by the qualified attachment we have to things in this world. These qualified attachments do not mean that we live at half energy and avoid commitments; however, they do mean that no single relationship, no one achievement, no optimal stage of development can finally make us complete. Those things in which we try to find salvation are our idols.

Experience should teach us how changing our patterns of life are. As children we believe our parents are superman and superwoman, and as we reach adulthood we are surprised to discover that they are only persons like ourselves. We may seek security in love, but sooner or later we discover that our partners are no more secure than ourselves. Then, we may hope for some permanence in our children only to realize that our children's lives are just as uncertain as our own. So it is too with our siblings, our friends, and our heroes. Human relationships are not absolute.

The fact that human relationships are not absolute does not imply that they are evil. Created for us, they are good gifts that enrich us. When, however, we allow human relationships to own us, they make us limited and small, and we destroy the Creator's good gifts. Loving God above all gives our love for our neighbor some limits and keeps it from dominating others and ourselves. When we give ourselves freely in life for God's sake, we become free and vital persons.

Because the creation is many-sided, we as persons are many-sided. Thus it is not only possible but also natural that in the course of her life a woman may be a daughter, wife, mother, neighbor, friend, citizen, and worker. Furthermore, she will not be the same in all of these roles, because each one brings to the fore a different set of possibilities for her. Healthy living is found in a life of many possibilities.

Healthy living is principled, it is governed by fidelity to God's intention for us, for others, and for life in this world. To discover, by living, what this means requires taking risks, doing our best, and trusting that God remains faithful. When we act in faith even mistakes, or conflicts, or disappointments cannot destroy the process of growth. Dietrich Bonhoeffer once wrote:

> God wants us to love him eternally with our whole hearts—not in such a way as to injure or weaken our earthly love, but to provide a *cantus firmus* to which the other melodies of life provide the counterpoint . . . Where the *cantus firmus* is clear and plain, the counterpoint can be developed to its limits . . . Only a polyphony of this kind can give life a wholeness and at the same time assure us that nothing calamitous can happen as long as the *cantus firmus* is kept going.[2]

Underwritten by the promise of God's faithfulness life is full of promise. Some women find it hard to believe that their own lives can be full of promise. They are confused because they live in a generation which is replacing old ways with new ways. These women know they will have to make choices, but they want some help to get hold of the problem and examine what the choices really are. This book is for them.

Mary Vander Goot

1

The Jumping Off Point

You wait little girl on an empty stage
For fate to turn the light on.
Your life little girl is an empty page
That men will want to write on . . .[1]

—from *The Sound of Music*

Just about every woman over the age of twenty can remember the time when *The Sound of Music* was a big hit. Stirred by the romance of the film, young women bought the soundtrack and played it until they knew the lyrics by heart. No one was offended by the handsome young fellow who sang these words to a very capable sixteen-year-old woman. But today, these words—which were once thought to be marvelously romantic—are called flagrantly sexist. Over the past decade and a half we have become familiar with the language of liberation.

We have also learned that it is often much easier to sound liberated than to live well. In fact, many women are genuinely confused about what being liberated really means. Are you liberated if you leave your husband? Get a job? Go back to school? Do Christian women need to be liberated?

The woman about whom and for whom this book is written is stuck in a confusing "liberation gap." She is an intelligent, middle-class woman between twenty and fifty, who is either still raising a family or whose children are beginning to grow up and leave the nest. She grew up in a time or in a family that didn't give much—if any—thought to liberation. Now, however, she finds herself living in a society that says if she's not liberated, she's not much. In trying to bridge the gulf that separates these extremes, she may have stopped fearfully on the edge, uncertain as to whether or even how to make a successful leap across. But, what is responsible action? What direction for the future will unfold the possibilities which God has given her?

The world in which we live prizes progress above all else. Thus old buildings are torn down to make way for new buildings, even though the old buildings may have been perfectly good or perhaps better than the new ones. In striving to be modern and up-to-date, our society often overlooks the basic worth of things it already has. This attitude spills over into our lives, and Christians are by no means exempt from it.

Although for centuries women were chastized when they attempted to vary from custom, today we are encouraged to "do our own thing" and get on with it. Thus the housewife is made to feel ashamed because she doesn't want to "get a job and fulfill herself," and the career woman is made to feel guilty for not spending more time at home with her family. Because of these enormous pressures to get on with it, we sometimes feel pushed to do what everyone else is doing. There does not seem to be enough time to think about the future—there's barely enough time to understand the present as it rushes by. Social pressure urges us to act now, before it's too late. But, how can we judge what is right and good for us unless we have some sense for how the present fits with the future and how our lives fit with the lives of others.

There is great danger in thoughtless action. If a woman lets herself be pushed to act before she is ready, she may just be imitating others rather than making the choices that are best for her. Getting a job or a divorce or a college education are not guarantees of liberation; nor are staying married or staying at home with the children necessarily impediments to liberation.

Because women were traditionally taught that the truly feminine woman adapts herself graciously to the will of others, the very thought of being assertive makes many women uneasy. Some women have reacted to what they see as the "bondage of traditional womanhood" with anger, refusing to bend to the wishes of others under any circumstances. This sort of "change" in a woman is not change at all—it's simply using the other side of the coin and calling it a new penny.

Learning to accept and adapt to change is particularly difficult for a woman who has launched herself into adult life without ever having given much thought to what lies ahead. This is as true for the career woman who thought her job would fulfill all of her needs as it is for the woman who believed getting married and raising a family would be a blissful life-time experience. Having made one change in their lives—leaving home for work or marriage—these women never expected to have to make any more major decisions. But like it or not, we cannot avoid change. Our children grow up; our spouses develop new interests; our jobs are not as challenging as they once were. Instead of recognizing the inevitability of change, however, many women put up obstacles to change—even denying that anything *has* changed. Thus they effectively stop their own growth. Until the obstacles are removed, they will be unable to mature.

This book is about change: learning to recognize it and to meet its challenges. It follows that a woman who decides to take responsibility for her own life needs to acquire the necessary tools for doing so, and she has to learn that making some choices in life matters. In this book you will learn that it is indeed possible to chart your own course in life, to make constructive choices, to plan a course of action, and to take that course to enrich your own life and the lives of those close to you, and especially to be responsible.

Sometimes this takes courage, especially if the move is an unfamiliar one or if you are not used to making such moves. But there is no need to be afraid: it is not necessary to "leave the world behind," break up your home, or quit your job. It also is not necessary to be reckless, irresponsible, or thoughtless of others. Deliberately moving ahead to become all that God has made possible for you is the most responsible and thoughtful way to live.

2

Where Are You Going?

"Oh, what tangled webs we weave . . ."

Our world is changing at an accelerating—indeed, an alarming—rate. Was it just ten years ago that the components of the computerized calculator you carry in your pocket were so large they had to be housed in an entire building? Has television really been with us for thirty years? And how can those same folks who used to tell us to hop in our cars and see America first, tell us it is our patriotic duty to stay close to home this summer and conserve energy? How is it possible to know what is right and proper in such a confusing world?

Of course the fact that others are just as confused as we are does not prevent them from giving us well-meaning advice. But sometimes we get so many opinions that it seems a lot easier to just let life take its course, whether or not we happen to like where the current is taking us.

And why not drift? Haven't women always drifted? Isn't it our right to be taken care of? It's true that just a few decades ago most women made few decisions about how they wanted to spend their lives. Their decisions were few because their options were few: girls were taught that they should grow up and get married, make a home, and raise children—period. They were sternly warned to exclude from their concerns anything that might interfere with their single-minded fulfillment of female destiny. Nineteenth-century folk wisdom taught that a woman who did not become a full-time mother was likely to suffer from a withered uterus, and on top of that she was probably neurotic and frigid. In other words, if a woman wanted to live her life differently, she was probably crazy and was certainly in for a bad time.

Over the past few decades, however, the status of women has changed. Feminist protests and the women's liberation movement countered this narrow doctrine of female destiny, and the status of women has gradually improved. Early protests secured a woman's right to own property, to transact business, and to vote; later demands were made for equal educational opportunity, equal pay for equal work, and nondiscriminatory hiring practices. Today efforts are being directed toward changing the damaging stereotypes of women as either sweet, helpless darlings or nagging shrews.

In years past, women who wanted to follow a conventional lifestyle had dozens of examples all around them. If at any point they were uncertain, needed advice, or did not know exactly what was expected of them, they had only to look around and imitate someone a bit older or more experienced. But the security of traditional patterns is no longer with us. A young girl going out on a date once had to worry about whether or not to kiss the boy. Now she has to decide who should pay, and if *she* should call *him* again. There are no longer any easy answers, and the maze of questions grows ever more bewildering.

It is becoming increasingly apparent that one thing we can count on is change. If a woman can accept change as natural, and work with it, she can live a rewarding life. But sometimes it seems as if our lives are changing and moving on without us. Faced with this frightening circumstance, many women feel that making a change—any change—is better than doing nothing at all. However, women who break out of the security of their traditional patterns give up the security of a relatively predictable life. They have to take risks; and if they make mistakes, they have to seek their own remedies. Twenty years ago in her book *The Feminine Mystique*, Betty Freidan said such decisions represent a "terrifying jumping-off point" for women.[1] And things haven't changed much since then. Furthermore, it is not oppression that engenders terror, but the uncertainty of a freedom without models to demonstrate its use.

Fortunately, there is no decision we can make that means choosing one pattern of life and foreclosing all others, although by making a choice we are implicitly choosing not to do something else. We will have to face many jumping-off points in our lives. A woman's first jumping-off point, for example, may have been a decision to put off college until after marriage and family were well started. Eventually she will have to deal with the question of whether or not she really wants to go back to school. One decision will not carry her through the rest of her life.

Women who have passed the first jumping-off point and formed some long-term personal commitments—to work, family, or home—feel even less comfortable than younger women do about venturing to change the patterns of their lives. Married women and mothers often feel guilty if they dream of future plans, because it seems an admission that they are not content with their lives the way they are. Questioning the validity of the traditional roles of wife and mother can stir up ugly worries about whether or not she is a deficient woman. Many women know very well the hurt and anger they feel on being told, when they suggest they would like to extend their lives beyond being a wife or mother, "Do you know what your problem is? You just don't like being a woman." Even women who are contented with the present are reluctant to plan for a time when circumstances will be different. They believe that the fact that they commited themselves to a lifestyle in early adulthood obligates them to stick with it.

Like it or not, our lives don't stay the same forever. No matter what sort of a life we have chosen or drifted into at our first jumping-off point, sooner or later we will come to a second one. If we accept this natural process and work with it, these times can be rewarding periods of growth. But if we try to deny the need for change, we may be headed into a fullblown crisis.

Three Crises

A Crisis of Preparation:
"I don't know how to do anything!"

"I don't know how I became an adult," laments Sue. "I waited around while other people made decisions for me, until finally everything was settled, and here I am. When I finished high school I took some secretarial courses and got a job. I think I was a pretty good secretary, but I didn't take it very seriously. I wanted to get married, and I figured that once I did, a job wouldn't be very important.

"But now I'm thirty-five, my children are growing up, and I want to do something. I don't have too much confidence, and nobody seems to give me much encouragement, either. I'm not sure what I want to do, or even what I could do, but to tell you the truth I'm bored with everything and I have to do something."

Sue never took a hand in planning her own life. Instead, she just lived from day to day and assumed she had no decisions to make. So now that she is beginning to feel empty, depressed, and restless, she doesn't know where to begin looking for ways to liven up her life. Worse, she has no real experience in decision-making, and lacks confidence in her own abilities. Sue is so bored that she's ready to make any change, even a drastic one, just to relieve the tension. If she were to do this, however, she would be just like a person who decides to take a vacation, but doesn't think about where to go until after the bags are packed and the taxi has started for the airport. This sort of action may be exciting for a few weeks, but it's certainly no way to plan a life.

A Crisis of Overcommitment:
"Do something else? I have too much to do already!"

"How can I even think of doing something new? My life is too full as it is! I've got all that I can handle, and there's not an inch of room for anything else. Anyway, who would do all this stuff if I just said, 'No more'? Sometimes I do feel a little hectic, as if I'm racing around doing a thousand things that don't add up to much. But there are people counting on me, and I can't let them down. What should I do, just say 'no'? I wish I could do some things that were just for myself, but I don't know how I'd fit them in."

Janet's crisis is the opposite of Sue's. Janet's life is full to capacity with commitments, and she has come dangerously close to exhausting her last resource. She's not alone in her problem, however. Women as a group tend to let their responsibilities expand to consume all of their time and use up all of their energy. In fact, women often take on responsibilities when there is no real reason to do so. Instead of learning to delegate, they become the "take-care-of" person in the family—the one who takes care of all the details that allow everyone else's life to run smoothly. Ironically, the same woman who tolerates this high pressure, low-satisfaction lifestyle would probably be the first to recognize it as unhealthy if she saw that her husband or children were living this way.

Janet may find herself "too busy" now, but as her children grow up she will find herself with less and less real work to do. If she continues to fill her time with meaningless details, she will find herself running in circles with no apparent way out.

A Crisis of Permanence:
"I'm afraid to rock the boat."

"I don't dare to change my life very much, because I don't want to end up losing what I've got. Better safe than sorry, you know. What if I rock the boat and end up losing everything? I admit I'm not happy, but a lot of women are worse off than I am. Anyway, I'm not the type to complain, and I'm not going to walk out on what I have. So I'd better just stop being selfish and try to be contented."

Mae mistakes stagnation for permanence, and feels any change as a threat. But Mae is in for some real surprises. She is unaware that the important things in her life will change, even if she does not. Is a twenty-year-old marriage the same as it was at the beginning? Of course not. Are eighteen-year-old children the same as they were at birth? It is fervently to be hoped that they are not! Can a time-worn job be full of the same challenges it had at the start? Not often. Things change, and Mae will too.

The Three Stages of a Relationship

Each of these women has options open to her, if only she were equipped to recognize them. Sue must learn how to take control of her own life back from other people; Janet must learn to let her family and friends take some responsibility away from her; and Mae must learn that it is possible to satisfy her own needs without denying others their needs. Each woman will have to stop drifting with the current and take control of her life. Just as it would be foolish to jump into the river if you did not know how to swim, it is equally foolish to try to make life decisions without having learned the basics.

To understand what the basics are, we need to learn something about the nature of relationships. We stand in some sort of relationship to each aspect of our lives—husband, children, parents, friends, vocation. The nature of each relationship is as subject to change as we are; and recognizing the need to move on with a relationship is a prerequisite to growth. Although most of our relationships are complex, they can be said to have three major stages: predisposition, immersion, and emergence.

Predisposition: Getting Prepared

"Bill and I are happy together, but sometimes I feel that something is missing from my life. I feel a little guilty saying this, but my marriage just isn't enough to make me happy anymore. I need something else, but I have no idea what it could be."

Even when your life is going smoothly, you may have a vague feeling of dissatisfaction with things as they are. Whether you know it or not, you are preparing yourself to do something new. Predisposition is unavoidable and nothing to feel guilty about, yet many women do feel guilty. Women who let this feeling overwhelm them may begin to feel helpless and depressed. But acknowledging our predisposition to change allows us to explore our needs and find out what we want to do with our lives. The stage of predisposition is especially valuable because it is an unpressured time we can use to make adequate preparations for the future. Just as you cannot build a stable house without a firm foundation, you cannot make mature and constructive decisions without taking the time to think them through.

Immersion: Getting Involved

"Ever since my son was born, I've spent all my time with him—playing with him, feeding him, making sure he's okay. Sometimes I wake up in the middle of the night even when he's not crying. It may seem like a lot of work to some people, and it is a lot more work than I'm used to, but I really love him and I don't mind. A lot of things I used to think were important don't mean as much to me now. My son is the most important part of my life."

When we are immersed in a new relationship, we are totally involved. Everything is seen as somehow related to the new interest, which takes center stage in our lives. The language of love—"I only have eyes for you"—is a vivid illustration of immersion. It is a period characterized by emotional exhilaration, new discoveries, and personal growth. The new relationship is often

allowed to displace those things or people we used to find important. We tend to stress the similarities between ourselves and our
new interest—"My boyfriend and I are exactly alike, we even like
the same flavor ice cream." As we will see later on, it is possible to
find yourself drawing in too much immersion; in order to progress,
it is necessary to understand emergence.

Emergence: Home Free

"In the last five years I've watched my son become an adult.
There's no doubt about it, his father and I grew up with him. We
would never have predicted he would become the person he is.
Still, I respect him for having his own way, and now I'm glad he
didn't just follow our wishes. He insisted on standing on his own
two feet. It wasn't easy to let him find his own way, but I don't
think we could have a good relationship if we didn't let him go."

When our involvement in the relationship levels off to a stable
and familiar plateau, it is called emergence. We emerge from the
relationship and look around to see the world with new eyes, and
we allow the relationship to leave center stage and assume its proper place in our lives. This does not mean that every relationship is
ultimately a failure and has to be discarded; on the contrary, it
means that if the relationship is to endure it must exist in propor-
tion to all of our other relationships. It is the lack of understanding
of this concept—the mistaken belief that when the romance is
gone, the relationship is over—that prevents many women from
making a healthy emergence. In contrast to immersion, which
stresses similarities, emergence helps us to appreciate the value of
individual differences: "My husband says he really likes it when I
work on my pottery, it gives him a chance to go fishing without
feeling guilty."

Discovering Where You Stand

Where do you stand? What aspects of your life are in
predisposition? Which need to be emerged? Which are in immersion? To begin life planning, you have to know where your life is at
the present, in what direction you would like it to move in the
future, and what you are going to do to set the process in motion.
Three simple steps? Probably not at first. At first glance, your life

may look like a hopeless mess, a jumble of tangled threads that will take forever to sort out.

But take a second look. Life planning is rather like sorting out the various threads that make up your life. Although it takes patience and hard work, there is a reward: you will finally be able to get a clear look at the pattern of your life, to see where the threads have come from, where they seem to be going, and, perhaps, what sorts of variations you can weave in the future. In Chapter Six you will have the opportunity to learn how to begin taking the knots out. But before taking up that tangled skein, it's important to understand just what you will be trying to accomplish.

3
What Is Change?

"My, how you've changed!"

—Anonymous

In a society where "change" and "growth" have become magic words, it's important not to make a change just for the sake of doing something different, or because others are making changes in their lives, or because there's nothing else to do. Changes in your life may be startling and dramatic, but they must be founded on a firm belief that creative planning is a way of discovering God's good gifts. In fact, if your new plans are not well-founded what you call "change" may really be more of the same old thing.

Immature Change

Conformist Change

Some women decide to get liberated because everyone else is doing it, and they don't want to feel left out. When women change their habits they may *look* as if they are becoming liberated: wife gets a job; husband takes over some of the household responsibilities; she learns to pound a nail; children learn to run the laundry equipment. But if all these changes are only a way of keeping up with the neighbors or doing what is in vogue, it represents little progress in terms of personal maturity. Women who change their habits in order to keep in style get caught in the bind of conformist thinking. Their basic motive is a

20

wish for approval, rather than a wish for real progress. This sort of "change" is deceptively easy and invites immediate gratification—there are always people around who will be flattered by imitation and will give approval to someone who thinks and acts the way they do.

But the sad fact is that a woman who "gets liberated" by attaching herself to new heroines or groups of heroines actually changes very little. She may receive her orders from a new source, but the old habit of following along with no questions asked remains a constant factor in her personality.

The conformist is easy to describe by caricature. Take Sandy, for instance. Once upon a time she was meticulous about her makeup, had her hair done every week, and bought the latest styles. Now she refuses to wear a speck of makeup, wouldn't dream of having a curler touch her hair, and wears blue jeans for most occasions. After all, what would her friends think? She used to read *Good Housekeeping* so she would know how to be "with it," she now reads *Ms.* for the same reason. If her friends make changes in their lives, she does too. When her husband makes a flattering remark about "those independent chicks at work," Sandy decides to be more independent. In payment for his newly liberated wife, her husband must chip in around the house—which means being especially helpful when they have company so her friends can see just how modern a couple they really are.

Conformist changing of roles goes smoothly in a neighborhood, suburb, or social group where a number of families are going through the same transition. We must not underestimate the social pressure on people to change under these circumstances. Unfortunately, conformist change accomplishes very little that is lasting. It may relieve the boredom for awhile, but once the novelty wears off the boredom sets in again. When a cause is new, anyone who rallies to it gets plenty of pats on the back for joining; but after a while new ways become old ways, the back-patting tapers off, and conformity is taken for granted. Without the compliments, the conformist loses all initiative to maintain the pattern.

Reactionary Change

Reactionary change is flip-flop thinking: I used to do that, therefore if I do the opposite I will have changed. Old heroes are turned into villains, good guys whom we once held to be unquestioned authorities are reclassified as bad guys who cannot possibly have good motives for anything. This is the style of "liberation" commonly found among women who feel that they have lived too long under the heavy hand of powerful authorities—typically their husbands, fathers, and bosses—and have been cheated out of their own lives. In desperation, they determine to break the stranglehold by resisting or negating everything they formerly revered.

Reactionary anger offers such women some momentary gain. For one thing, it allows them to vent a lot of anger. Women who disobey rules to show that they are not under the control of a particular person or group of persons get some hostile satisfaction from doing so. That's what happened to Betty, who after fifteen years of pampering her husband suddenly decided she'd had enough. Instead of discussing her new feelings with him, however, she just woke up one morning and refused to do anything for him unless his request recognized her option to refuse. One morning her husband left a note on the breakfast table that read, "Betty, my blue suit is at the cleaners and I need it for tomorrow." Betty knew from past experience that her husband assumed she would pick up the suit. She saw her opportunity, and—determined to break with the past—left the note on the table. When her husband came home from work, he was surprised to find a smug wife and no suit.

"You can't assume that just because you need something done I'll automatically do it for you," she told him. Indignantly she added, "You didn't even bother to say, 'Would you *mind* picking up my suit for me?'" He argued angrily that Betty was obviously the person to do the errand, because she had free time during the day while he had none.

The result of this incident and others like it was that Betty and her husband each felt mistreated by the other. Betty was convinced that her husband was a taskmaster who wanted her to be his slave, while he was convinced that Betty, for some unknown reason, was determined to make his life miserable. Neither would get behind the hurts to discuss reasonably how they might revise their responsibilities toward and expectations of each other.

This pattern may seem familiar to you, and for good reason:

two-year-olds use this same tactic of reactionary independence. When their parents say yes, they say no; and when their parents say no, they say yes. This stubborn attitude accomplishes something very important: they discover that they and their parents have separate wills. Once children feel quite certain about having their own wills, they use it to take some control over their own behavior. (Becoming toilet trained is one of the first indications of this control.) Similarly, adult women who realize they have meekly lived by someone else's agenda for too long are not sure they even have a mind of their own any more, and so they try out their wings in reactionary ways to prove that they are no longer intimidated by other people's expectations. Once they have proved their independence, they can begin to tolerate a correlation between their own good judgment and the wishes of others.

The need for freedom of choice is a key factor in the reactionary style of liberation. When people feel that their freedom of action is threatened, they may react in extreme ways to restore it. Such behavior, however, not only builds up bravado, it also builds up resistance in others that may only add to the woman's original feelings of being a victim. Rather than helping her out of her rut, then, her reactionary behavior may only propel her into a vicious circle of power struggles.

Sometimes acting in order to make a point may compel us to go through with something we dislike intensely just so we will not have to concede the point. Florence, after raising a large family, decided to go back to college. Her family and friends told her that at her age, fifty, it would be silly to pursue an education she couldn't use and didn't need. She was nevertheless determined to go to school, if only to prove something to herself; but she went to school with the doubts of others trailing along behind her. At midterm she realized that one of her courses was a deadly bore and not at all useful to her. But when she considered dropping the course, the warnings of her family and friends echoed in her ears. Rather than hear them say "I told you so," she ended up sitting out the class and wasting her time.

Another danger of reactionary thinking is that in fighting one evil we may go to the opposite extreme and woo another. Partially because for so long women were deemed incapable of doing much more than raising a family, the "superwoman" notion has recently gained popularity. According to this theory, every woman is capable of everything. This concept ignores the fact that everyone has limitations of one sort or another, and this kind of thinking often results in a woman blaming others for her limitations. I might argue, for example, that I cannot be a brain surgeon because no one has faith in me. As long as I can blame others for not believing in me, I do not have to consider honestly whether or not I have the skills or abilities to be a good brain surgeon.

Finally, reactionary behavior invites harmful stress. If our actions are disapproved by others, and especially if we intentionally provoke that disapproval, the stakes for success or failure become very high. Success may be a real ego boost, but failure is a terrible humiliation. Under these circumstances, when a whisper of self-doubt surfaces it quickly gets amplified into a warning shout of potential and humiliating failure. Is support available now? No, because it has been alienated by reactionary quarrels. Unless it is replaced by new support, the reactionary is forced to stand alone.

Power struggles may be a good way to make the loud and clear announcement, "Hey folks, I'm due for a change, so don't expect too much of the same old thing from me." Stating anger is sometimes a much healthier thing to do than bottling it up and turning it into ulcers, migraines, or alcoholism. As a long-term strategy for living, however, anger consumes too much energy and is not constructive. A woman who is spending all of her time watching for the enemy does not have any time or inclination to build forward-looking plans.

Add-on Change

Dramatic changes do not easily fit into settled ways. One means of avoiding the unsettling effect of changing old roles is to add on new ones. This strategy is analogous to building a new room onto your house and furnishing it independently of the rest. Emotionally, it means having several domains in your life, each of which you must keep distinct from the other.

The advantage of changing by adding on is that it allows you to try something new without rocking the boat. The new role is like a pilot study, it lets you take some risks without risking everything. Such add-on change, however, it not ideal. It only works as long as the old and new roles are kept separate. The moment you find yourself in both roles at once, confusion arises. For example, the mother who sees herself as an independent businesswoman at work may resent a phone call from her child during business hours, because it blurs the fragile line between her two identities.

Living in two separate domains does not, of course, require that you be phony in one of them. For example, you may be motherly with your children and professional at work; you need not be motherly with people at work or professional with your children. Nevertheless, you must have a solid grip on your self-understanding to keep the roles clear. No one else is going to do that for you. Somehow, you have to keep a firm connection between who you are and how each of these two roles is a true expression of yourself. If either of them is contrived, an imitation of someone else, or an ego trip based on false values, it will weaken the solid center of your personality that allows you to hold the multiple roles together.

Gretchen is an example of a woman who lives out her life in many sectors. She's a responsible executive at work, and at home her husband expects her to take care of his needs as well as their children's needs. Her parents still tend to treat her like their little girl, even though she's thirty-eight. Her dream, which follows, illustrates those bewildering feelings that erupt when one is in the process of bringing many identities together.

"I dreamed I had to appear in court, and when I arrived there I was stunned to see that it was full of people I knew. My husband and children were there, and my parents, my brothers and sisters, my co-workers, and even some of my neighbors. The visitors' gallery was full, and I knew everyone there.

"Before I took the stand, the bailiff came toward me, and I gathered it was so that I could take the oath. But he asked me if I had anything to say before taking the stand. I had the feeling that *I* was on trial. I tried to think if there was anything I should say. The only thing that came to mind was, 'My goodness, I don't know who I am!' I said that. The whole courtroom was silent. I wanted to run out but I couldn't move."

When all the different portions of Gretchen's life (represented by the people in the visitors' gallery) confront her at once in her dream, she feels she is on trial and doesn't know who she is. How does a mature woman cope with this confusion? How can she be true to all her loyalties? There is no simple answer. The only mature solution is to work hard at preserving the true character of each of these loyalties while holding them all in careful balance.

Change Toward Maturity

Each of the patterns discussed thus far focuses primarily on outward behavior, and each can pass as a form of change in as much as it involves breaking out of an old pattern. There is, however, a pattern of change which, although less dramatic, is more profound and lasting. A crash diet will often provide quick weight loss, but the pounds seldom stay off for long. When you change your basic approach and attitude toward food, the weight comes off more slowly but it comes off for good. By analogy, thorough change is slower change.

Such a pattern of change must come about in the course of emotional maturation. The mature woman has a strong idea of what she wants from her life, and this strength underlies her actions. She is more than liberated; she is wise. She knows that to build a stable house she must first build a strong foundation. Because each woman is unique and has her own special needs and ways of relating to the world, each woman's blueprint for life will be different—there is no one road to maturity. There are, however, some basic tools that every woman can learn to use. These are the art of self-respect, the art of finding support, and the art of dreaming.

The Art of Self-Respect

In my work as a psychologist, I have had many women tell me that they cannot get on with the business of life. Their complaints are usually one of two types. Complaint number one says, "The reason I can't get on with the business of life is because my parents never expected anything of me. That made me feel like they didn't think I was much, and they didn't love me very much." Complaint number two says, "The reason I can't get on with the business of life is that my parents expected too much of me. I didn't think I could ever measure up to their standards, so I stopped trying." Whether too much or too little was expected of them, these women all felt that because they weren't loved for what they were, no strings attached, they were unprepared for life.

In *The Art of Loving,* Erich Fromm describes two kinds of love that parallel these problems. Fromm calls one style motherly love, and the other fatherly love. Motherly love, he suggests, is affection experienced without conditions. It is not given as a reward, and it cannot be controlled. It is simply given by the mother to the child because the child is hers. As Fromm says, *"I am loved for what I am,* or perhaps more accurately, *I am loved because I am."*[1] By contrast, fatherly love is conditional, and can be gained or lost depending on whether the child meets the father's standards. Motherly love is passive love: you get it by the mere fact of your existence. Fatherly love is active love: you can control it by being obedient.

These two styles of affection have become confused in the experience of some daughters. In many families, the father is absent, either physically or emotionally, from the home. While he puts in some duty appearances for his son—after all, as they say, every boy needs his father—he deserts his daughter emotionally and leaves her to her mother. As the mother attempts to be all to the daughter, she ends up being both the conditional and unconditional sources of affection. Unfortunately, it is not easy to live with the two faces of Mom, and in the movement toward liberation the two-faced Mom has come under attack as second only to men in the ranks of oppressors.[2]

Thus the love-hate relationship so many daughters form with their mothers grows out of this mixture of conditional and unconditional affection. Mothers, it seems, switch back and forth between the two styles, and their pattern of making these switches is not always well-matched to their daughters' needs. The same mother who at one moment accepts her daughter unconditionally becomes conditional in her love for her daughter when she trains her to be "feminine." If her daughter fails to be "what women are supposed to be," the mother withdraws her love and the daughter feels guilty. To resolve this tension, most daughters learn to be passive. Simone de Beauvoir describes such a relationship in her autobiography:

> And that is how we lived, the two of us, in a kind of symbiosis. Without striving to imitate her, I was conditioned by her . . . I learned from Mama to keep in the background, to control my tongue, to moderate my desires, to say and do exactly what ought to be said and done. I made no demands on life, and I was afraid to do anything on my own initiative.[3]

If mother's love were the only thing women needed in life there would be no problem. There is, however, more to life than mother. Moreover, the strategy that works with her does not work when we try to apply it elsewhere, and that is where the frustration arises. When women break out of their passivity, they become angry at their mothers. "She never expected anything of me. She didn't respect me. She never thought I was worth anything." At the same time they say, "I never felt I could really please her. I don't know what she wanted of me, but whatever it was I didn't match up." The anger a daughter feels toward her mother is provoked by the disappointment the daughter feels toward herself. She feels that she should have been, but never was, taught self-respect by her mother. She may, however, be wrong.

Parental affection is a model for self-respect: the two styles in which our parents love us represent the two sides of self-respect. Therefore healthy self-love is both conditional and unconditional. If you respect yourself unconditionally, for example, you are able to say, "No matter what, I'll never give up on myself." At the same time, conditional self-love allows one to say, "What I do makes a difference. I'm not satisfied to do just anything, I want to do the best I can." These two forms of self-respect depend on and complement each other. Without conditional self-respect, unconditional self-respect loses its potency. That is, if what I do makes no difference, I feel apathetic and depressed. On the other hand, if all my self-respect is conditional, my courage may fail me because I'm not perfect, and why should I attempt to do something if I know I'll never get it right? Only when the two sides are in healthy balance is it possible to be productive without fear of failure. Then it is also possible to believe that your efforts make a difference, and that your failures are not the end of the world.

Parents are the first people with whom we experience the two kinds of affection that are woven together in self-respect. However, if by adulthood the basics of self-love have not been learned, no woman needs to despair. Few of us have the two sides of self-respect in perfect balance. Some of us have an exaggerated need to perform and earn approval, others of us have a lingering need to be loved without conditions. In adulthood we all still need to have sources of both conditional and unconditional approval to reinforce our self-respect, but these sources no longer need to be our parents.

Each of us needs to assess our own balance of self-respect in order to understand in which direction the balance is tipped. Once we know what we lack, we also know what to ask for. Unfortunately, we are often afraid to ask for the affection we need. What if our requests seem childish? What if we ask the impossible? What if we are refused? All of these risks are compounded if we think that one person must fill all of our needs for approval, and women seem particularly prone to expecting that one person will supply all of their emotional needs. Perhaps the women who once believed their mothers could do this, but then discovered they could not, look for another single source as a substitute. First they turn to their husbands—but only to find that what their mothers could not do, their husbands cannot do either. After their husbands, they turn to their children, and here too they are disappointed.

We need not be afraid to turn next to ourselves, and we need not be afraid to get the backing we need for our self-love. If we seem childish, all the better; children have the gift of candor in seeking what they need. If we ask for something specific, it is not likely to be impossible. And if we are refused we can ask someone else. The best way to balance our self-respect is by testing the case. If we need to strengthen one side of this respect, we should find someone else to help us.

Assurances of unconditional affection can be gotten by asking. There is probably no one in the world who will accept us absolutely, one hundred percent, no matter what. There are persons, however, whose conditions can be met with relative ease. If you need to know how openly accepted you are, ask. For example, find a friend you can trust and ask, "Would you like me better if I was prettier? Would you like me better if I were more intelligent? Would you like me better if I weighed ten pounds less?" In all likelihood you will find that others are more accepting of you than you are of yourself. Although they may not give perfect unconditional approval, they can help you along.

Asking for conditional approval works in much the same say. For example, if you feel uncomfortable in social situations, ask a friend to give you some reflections about yourself. Ask if you are too aggressive or too shy, too talkative or too quiet, too serious or too silly. When you see these reflections of yourself in someone else's mirror, you can make some judgments about yourself and build up your conditional self-respect.

The Art of Getting Support

One of the reasons women do not get the help they need is that they look for it in the wrong places. Sometimes women assume that their families—in whom they have invested most of their energy—must be able to offer all of the encouragement, understanding, and support that they need for new ventures. These women forget that, because our families are closely involved in what happens to us, the times during which we need encouragement are times during which our families themselves need reassurance. We may think it unfair that our loved ones, whom we have always encouraged, do not back our ventures; but, fair or not, that is life. Sometimes our families are too close to us to be able to give us the backing we need.

Consider this example. When a mother with little children goes on a family vacation, she is often busier away from home than she is at home. Living out of suitcases and adjusting to unfamiliar places is a strain on the organizer. Even when parents evenly divide the work of childcare, there is enough to keep both parents occupied most of the time. Furthermore, most mothers have taken on the role of psychological parent to a greater extent than fathers have. This means that father can walk out of the room with the statement, "I'm going out to get a newspaper," while a mother would say, "I'm going out to get a newspaper. Will you watch the kids?"

This mother, after a perfectly usual and pleasant family vacation, might come home wishing she could take a vacation by herself next time. A vacation alone would mean no one but herself to supervise, plan for, and entertain. If she says this to her family, however, they may very well think she did not enjoy their company, that they misbehaved in some way, and that the vacation was a failure. If she expects her family to understand her dream of going on vacation by herself, she is likely to be disappointed. They will meet her suggestion with hurt looks, and she will feel guilty.

If a mother who comes home tired from a vacation wants to try out her idea on someone who can understand, she should share it with another tired mother who has just returned from a perfectly happy family vacation. Friends can sometimes understand our need for a change of agenda, because they do not take our complaints personally. Furthermore, it is understood that when we go to a friend with a problem or a complaint, our friend does not have to solve the problem or correct the complaint. All the friend has to do is hear us out. A friend's responsibility is different from that of a woman's family.

Women can also find important support in a mentor—someone who has already been down the road we choose to take, and has gained some wisdom from the experience. Do you want to know what happens if you go back to school at age forty? Ask someone who has. Do you want to know what happens when children grow up and the nest is empty? Find someone who seems to have handled that transition well. Ask her how she did it. If you don't already know such women, ask your friends and keep your eyes and ears open.

When live mentors cannot be found, surrogate mentors may provide a source of encouragement. These are often found in books, and especially in autobiographies. Groups may also serve as mentors. In some places women have formed groups to provide a support system for each other. For example, the Boston Health Collective began as an effort on the part of women who felt they needed other women for support. They found their venture so productive that they gathered their ideas into a book. The book sold well and eventually paved the way for a second book by the same group. In the preface to their first book, *Our Bodies, Ourselves*, these women wrote:

> We talked to each other about what it was like for us, growing up female. The underlying purpose of this introspection and analysis of our past was to have some basis for figuring out how we wanted to change the ways we thought and felt about ourselves . . . To do this very personal work we made an accepting environment for ourselves—a place where we could talk and work together and think out loud.[4]

Women must rid themselves of the notion that going outside of the family to find support is a betrayal of the family. It is unrealistic to expect that children and husbands understand the lives of mothers and wives if these women are having difficulty understanding their lives themselves. Turning again and again to husband and children only to find that they cannot offer needed encouragement breeds bitterness. Such women may think that their persistence is a form of loyalty, but loyalty to a myth is not a virtue. Women can get the encouragement they need if they are willing to find out who has it to give. We need to discover, but not to dictate, who will support us and how. Getting the help we need is truly a fine art.

The Art of Dreaming

Good predispositions take time to grow, and we grow them best when we grow them well in advance. Women have long had the reputation for being dreamers. If they are indeed dreamers, then this is one of their strengths. Unfortunately, the remark to the effect that women are dreamers has often been tossed off as a criticism or as a warning that women need not be taken seriously. There is also a grain of truth in this criticism: women must learn to capitalize on their dreams to the extent that they will be able to act on them.

We can think of our dreams as running along a line that goes from barely formed dreams to confident actions. Far in advance of predisposition, then, there is a fantasy. In fantasy we can play with ideas, we can imagine actions, we estimate the advantages and disadvantages, and we can do this with few personal costs. As the old saying goes, dreams are free. The flexibility of dreams invites us to be our creative best. Let me give an example of my own dreams. Someday I would like to learn to fly a glider and write a novel. To me, writing a novel is more realistic than learning to fly a glider, but flying is probably more of an adventure than writing a novel. In my fantasy, I play with both dreams because they balance each other well.

I do not know if I will ever write a novel, but that is not important now. If I were to start tomorrow, I am sure my novel would be a disaster. In fact, I probably wouldn't get past the first five pages. It is not even likely that I could write a novel in the next five years because my dreams need that long, if not longer, to ferment. Furthermore, anywhere along the line I can give up that dream if the idea loses its appeal for me.

Having a dream about writing a novel has caused a certain focus of attention for me. Whenever I run across something written about novelists, I read it. Sometimes the information is just a scrap—a five-line comment in a magazine book review—at other times the information is more extensive—a biography or a personal journal. At one time I read John Steinbeck's account of how he wrote *East of Eden*. I was so intrigued by it that I passed it on to a friend. Sometime later my friend apologetically returned the book with the admission that he had not finished it because he found it a deadly bore. I guess we must have different dreams. I do not read about novelists as a form of discipline; I read about them because I am entertained by this kind of reading.

Who knows what the next steps of my dream will be? Perhaps I will find a mentor who will start injecting some realistic facts about styles, publishers, and techniques into my thinking. Already now I hear about people or events and think that certain character types or certain profoundly human situations would make interesting material. Maybe next I will start writing some of these tidbits down. Almost certainly my way of talking about my dream will change. These days I say, "Sometimes I have this far-out fantasy that I would like to write a novel." What could be more tentative than that? When I find myself saying, "If I write a novel . . ." or "In the novel I would like to write . . ." I'll know my dream is beginning to take a more definite shape. That gradual change in my language is a way of sharing my dream with others and perhaps a step in actualizing it for myself.

In all honesty I must admit that novel-writing is still something that other people do. Probably I will never write one. Maybe I will learn to fly a glider instead. We all drop plenty of dreams along the way, but if we take ourselves seriously we continue to make new ones. Dreams are a way of getting predispositions started. It is easy to forget about predispositions when we are busily involved in the present. However, if we wait until we need a new venture before we start dreaming up a predisposition, it may be too late. Good predispositions take time to grow, and taking charge of our own predispositions also means learning the art of good timing.

In summary, changing is not something that can be done quickly or superficially. It involves an examination and perhaps a reassessment of all our deepest feelings and most ingrained habits. If we are used to acting passively or immaturely, then our so-called changes will also be passive or immature attempts, and will probably leave us in the same old rut. If you despair of ever changing, remember that you have been used to your old habits for a long time. It is unrealistic to believe that, through sheer force of will, old patterns can be changed overnight. In changing yourself, you are giving birth to a new person. Has anyone ever told you that giving birth was easy?

4
Predisposition: Thinking Ahead

"On your mark, get set . . ."

You may be surprised to find that predisposition to new ideas often occurs just when existing relationships are well established and our lives are stable. In fact, it is this very stability that enables us to move forward. The urge to grow and do different things with our lives is natural—indeed, it is virtually unavoidable. Taking charge of your life means first taking charge of your predispositions: acknowledging them, exploring them, and giving them room to grow.

Some women feel that they don't have any predispositions—they're not happy with their lives, but there doesn't seem to be anything else to do. They can't envision a future that's any brighter than the bleak present. Such women typically feel that even if they wanted to do things differently, they wouldn't be able to because (1) they don't think they could, (2) others don't think they could, or (3) they think that others don't think they could. Confused? Think how they feel! They're living under the burden of false expectations. To some extent we all do that. How did we get stuck with these expectations, anyway?

Expectations: What am I supposed to do?

Although we have inherited some of society's expectations for us, we are not stuck with them. To bleat helplessly is not only

34

useless, it is a refusal to see that the burden of change rests with us. If you remain passive, not much will happen to change your old predispositions. No fairy godmother will wave a magic wand to change society and make everything rosy. If you take charge of your life, you must expect some people to tell you that you are making them unhappy, that you are failing your family, or that you do not know your place as a woman. In the end, you will have to be honest about your motives and then trust your own judgment.

No-Fault Expectations

Who has all these expectations of us? Could it be that in childhood we learned to do only what others wanted? I doubt that. Once I became a parent I realized that even a newborn has a will of its own. Although my infants were dependent on me, I never got the impression that they were putty in my hands, desperately trying to please me. I usually got quite the opposite impression. For the first few months of life it was themselves they tried to please, as I attempted to learn from their sounds and actions ways in which I might keep them happy.

Modern psychology—probably because it is addressed to parents rather than to infants—has left us with the impression that parents are completely in charge of what happens to their children emotionally. We tend to think that parents act deliberately while the little ones just respond. At the same time, however, parents discover that no baby is entirely passive. Most babies are hard to figure out, and even so-called "easy babies" have their own ways and a certain stubborn insistence on doing things as and when they wish. Wise parents do their best to pattern a level of compatibility that suits both the infant and themselves.

This phenomenon should be of interest to those women who, "after the liberation," think back on their experience as daughters. Women's liberation has encouraged women to take responsibility for their lives and free themselves from the past. In reacting to the past, however, many women assume that their personal history is something that was done *to* them, and with which they had little to do. They think they have been victimized all along.

In trying to understand our origins, we often go about asking questions in the manner of a detective solving a mystery. We try to crack the riddle of our families, our parents, and our society: "My mother was too insecure, that's why I . . ." "I never got as much as my brother did, so of course . . ." "There's no opportunity for women in this country, so I never . . ." But we forget to ask the most important question: What kind of child was I?

We must depend on others for memories of our first stages, because those events go back beyond the boundaries of our memories. This is not a disadvantage, however. It is good for us to hear the reports of our childhood from someone else. For example, no one knows better than our parents that, as infants, they could not make us into whatever they wanted us to be. They do not believe that they designed us into the infants we were, nor do they believe that they made us into the adults we have become. We had our own peculiar ways and they had to learn to live with us. They had no more power over us than we have over our own children. Indeed, experiencing these limits with our children can help us listen honestly to our story and stop feeling like victims.

The point here is not to shift blame from parent to infant, but to get out of the blaming rut altogether. Once we do this, we cannot blame someone else for what we are. Why should we encourage our parents to feel guilty for things that were beyond their control? For example, I am reminded of Vera, who told me apologetically that she never cuddled her youngest daughter very much. This particular baby seemed most content to lie flat on her mother's lap, and she resisted being held snugly in her mother's arms or cuddled over her mother's shoulder. Vera felt guilty because she was sure her daughter had not gotten her cuddle quota. What she overlooked is that her daughter gave every indication of not wanting to be cuddled.

Coming to consciousness means not only that we gather some information about our past experience, but also that we do it in a more realistic manner than just sorting out our heroes and villains. Heroes did not make our virtues, nor did villains make our faults. If we cannot gain more productive insights than this we will only gain some new scapegoats, and continue being as childish as ever. If we want to take responsibility for ourselves as adults, we can begin by accepting our past experiences as really ours. In many cases, we gain new respect for our own independence if we can retrieve impressions of ourselves from the early stages of our lives, before we chose the way of feminine passivity.

Early impressions can usually be gotten by any woman who

wants them. A most obvious source is parents, but where that is not possible a sibling, an aunt or uncle, or someone a little older who was on the scene will have something to offer. It is, however, necessary to ask the questions well. Any woman who comes striding in like a constable with a search warrant, determined to hunt out fugitives and bring justice, will not be likely to get an accurate picture. Similarly, the beleagured, self-pitying daughter who comes asking questions to determine if things have always been so bad will leave with empty assurances that things used to be better. Important questions, it is good to remember, have to be asked proddingly and several times. Precious sources of information have to be reassured that it is not a nice story but the truth that is sought. To seek out your past, you may have to be bold and patient.

Getting down to roots almost always results in a remodeling of memories. First, we discover that not all of society wants to put us in a strait-jacket. At best, there is a handful of persons whom we do not want to disappoint. Second, when we meet those persons face to face and ask what it is they really want from us, we are surprised that we have exaggerated and distorted their expectations. Third, we have to learn to discriminate between what others expect of us and what we expect of ourselves. Sometimes it is our own expectations that are the most burdensome. Once we have sorted out which expectations belong to whom, whether or not we should fulfill them becomes clearer.

Regardless of what people expect, every standard of behavior to which we comply is ultimately our own. Originally, someone else may teach us the standard—a schoolteacher may teach that it is not ladylike to argue—but as long as that expectation belongs only to someone else, it does not affect us. If and when we comply, it is for reasons of our own. Once we make a habit of complying, the rule is our rule along with the responsibility for its keeping. We are not helplessly determined by outside influences.

Becoming an adult requires that we learn to scrutinize not only what others expect of us, but more important, if we are to become mature we must be aware of our own motives and expectations. To evaluate these expectations means to take charge of our old predispositions and our reasons for action. It also involves the realization that although we may not be able to change all of the expectations that others have for us, we can choose whether we want to live up to these expectations. As we do that, we become responsible to and for ourselves.

How to Re-Form Traditional Expectations

Women who were raised traditionally begin with a limited set of predispositions—wife and mother—and many of these women never evaluate or change these predispositions. Instead they passively accept what others plan for them, and go on living by that agenda. This unquestioning acceptance of stereotyped roles eventually leads to apathy, powerlessness, and defeat. It is not the roles of wife and mother *per se*, but the passivity with which they are accepted that is a block to maturity. This block continues to trap women in the "liberation gap."

Once adolescence is past it is more difficult to make the transition from childhood dependence on others to adult self-determination. But even though it is more difficult, it is never too late. When women shift from passive acceptance to active self-determination, they find that the persons who have always managed women's lives do not welcome the change. Traditional-minded husbands, parents, even children do not welcome a woman's new assertiveness. Women struggling for self-determination are made to feel silly, troublesome, selfish, or pushy.

Take Beth, for example, a married woman who after some years of seemingly contented married life began to ask herself how she got where she is. As she surveyed her life, she realized that it was her parents and her husband—more than herself—who wanted her to marry. Because she had no outstanding reason to veto the plan, she quietly went along with their wishes. When pressed to account for why she had not just said "no" when her husband asked her to marry him, Beth claimed that he'd never really asked. After they had known each other for some time, he surprised her with a diamond. In a romantic moment, he slipped it on her finger, and before she could say a word he had sealed the arrangement with a kiss. Once the diamond was on her finger they only talked about when, not if they should marry. Thus her decision to get married was not really her decision at all.

When Beth tried to explain to her husband that she regretted never having made up her own mind, he was offended. His retort was to ask her if she had married him against her wishes or if she thought she could have done better. When she tried to explain that he had missed the point, he replied that as far as he could see her only point was to make trouble. They left it at that because she felt too awkward to pursue her point further, but she had clearly gotten the message once again that thinking for herself was not necessary as long as she had someone to think for her. That, however, no longer satisfied her. Beth realized, although her husband did not understand, that the way a decision is made is as important as the decision itself—one affects the other. She resolved in the future to begin taking a hand in her own decisions.

Learning to Make Active Decisions

The way in which we make decisions parallels the way we live them out. Active decisions we live out actively, and passive decisions we live out passively. If we are in charge, we feel genuine satisfaction for each bit of progress we achieve; but the delight is often missing if someone else has decided for us what we are going to do. When we are in charge, we feel the press of the situation and stick with it even when things do not go well. We feel obliged to do something about consequences that are our own. But our responsibility is not so clear when we are swept passively along on someone else's agenda. Then we can easily step back and blame the planner.

Once we choose a major course of action, we commit ourselves to a whole series of further decisions that come up along the way as a result of the first choice. The example of the decision to marry serves to make this point. The initial decision to marry is necessarily followed by many day-to-day deliberations about how these two people can stay happily married to each other. Making all of these decisions at one time is impossible. What can be partially determined in advance, however, is the way in which decisions will be made.

The style of decision-making in marriage is formed early, and the same strategies are repeated each time husband and wife face a choice. The woman who floats into marriage passively will probably be passive in daily decisions as well. Instead of asking herself what she must do to keep her marriage healthy, she only asks what she must to do keep her husband happy. Because she does not respect her own interests, she gradually begins to feel that she does not own her marriage, but simply plays at it for the sake of others.

Women who do not take responsibility for their lives slowly become disillusioned and in middle age often burst forth in rage. They see that they have trusted others, but feel cheated on the returns they received for their trust. They want to scream out at everyone close to them, "I went your way, I bent to your wishes, I spent myself for you, but you don't care, you don't pay back, you don't love me!" This rage is laced with self-righteousness: "I served you and you made me a victim." It erupts in tirades of blaming: "I've let you have your way and you've ruined everything." But in the end the anger collapses into feelings of worthlessness: "I deserve better, but I've gotten nothing and I am nothing."

To love such blaming and angry women is not easy. And, unfortunately, there is no immediate cure. Those close to them feel guilty because there is an element of truth in their rage, but these "oppressors" also feel duped because the women went along with the injustice so happily. Why did they wait until now to protest? Why did they wait so long to speak for their own interests? The sooner women can begin expressing their own feelings, the less likely they are to end up mired in rage.

The Problem of Being Over-Prepared. Women drift along in marriage and motherhood because they are over-prepared for these roles. They are thoroughly indoctrinated with the idea that they must be wives and mothers, but they are not taught that before they assume these roles and form styles of life around them they must rethink their own predispositions. When such gaps are left in our training, we are forced to fill them ourselves. If we don't, overpreparation easily turns into conformity.

Ingmar Bergman in his film *Scenes From a Marriage* embodies this problem in the character of Marianne. Throughout her entire girlhood she was taught to get along with others, and be compatible and agreeable. She is so well-trained that when her husband finally leaves her, she is utterly confused. With no one to please, with no one to tell her what is wanted, she does not know how to be. In the film she writes a long journal entry, which she reads to her husband on one of his visits. Pouring out her deepest feelings of regret, she recalls all of the pressures she felt to conform. Finally, in a wrenching statement of her personal misery, she says:

So it has gone on and on. In my relations with other people. In my relations with men . . . The same desperate attempts to please everyone. I have never thought: What do I want? But always: What does *he* want me to want?[1]

Her confession complete, Marianne looks up to discover her husband sound asleep. Marianne is the woman who has been programmed for marriage. When finally she accomplishes her goal, she knows only how to pretend. Her training has been so thorough that she knows no other way to act.

Ironically, it is women who have spent the least amount of time dreaming about marriage who are in many respects the best prepared for it. Dreaming is a pastime for young women who are waiting, biding their time, with nothing else to do. Women who are not over-prepared with grandiose expectations for marriage are busy doing other things that give them a valuable fund of experience. This experience, in turn, rescues them from the trap of just waiting for the "magic moment." They are lucky women who are prepared for adulthood as well as marriage.

The Problem With Being too Tentative. Waiting plays into the pattern of female passivity that keeps women immature. It trains women not to expect that they can do anything to make their lives active, constructive, and absorbing. Even among college women who are training for professions and have promising futures, the hazards of waiting are often apparent. Their career plans are full of "ifs" because they try to stay ready at all times to adapt their careers to marriage.

The tentative quality of women's plans shows itself in the language women use when talking about their careers. A woman is more likely to say "I *might try* teaching," while a man will say "I *am going* into teaching." A woman will say "I *would like* to be an accountant," but a man says "I *am going* to be an accountant." Women add "ifs" and "maybes" because they stand ready to make concessions about which most men never even think.

Before the attitude of gamblers' luck can be removed from women's predispositions for marriage, it will be necessary to get rid of the old courtship patterns that leave everything up to men. When women can be as active as men in choosing when and whom to marry, then marriage will become a healthier institution for women. That means women must be free to seek the acquaintance of interesting men, and to pursue relationships with them.

Men have always had this privilege, and consequently have not had to endure the panic of being passed over or the danger of holding out until there are few eligible partners remaining. If women become more definite and less tentative, they will not feel compelled to find men who are older or higher in status than they are. We know that age and status give power and authority in most human relationships. As long as women feel they must marry men with the advantages of emotive power based on age and rank and the right to do all the asking, women are setting themselves up to be monopolized by marriage.

Young women often ask with some impatience how long they will have to wait until the old courtship patterns change. The question indicates that these women are still waiting, and doing so unaware that they will only have to wait as long as they choose to wait. All it takes to change the pattern is to break the rule. Don't be tentative, be definite! A man who cannot handle that is probably not the kind of man with whom a woman with life plans needs to seek further acquaintance anyway.

Forming New Predispositions for Motherhood. Being a mother is a profound experience, but it also involves risks. Most of us were taught to expect the profundities, but few of us were prepared to handle the risks. As little girls we were introduced to the longing of the good queen in *Snow White*, who sat by the window and watched the snowflakes feather down while she dreamt to herself, "If only I had a child . . ." Motherhood was her obsession. With a child she believed she would be complete; without a child she would be nothing.

Romantic motherhood is not sensible, it is suicidal: a woman who thinks that motherhood will be the only and eternal wellspring for her future happiness is sure to be disappointed. When she is tired, distracted, or in need of company other than that of children, she will feel guilty. She will wonder secretly if she is an emotional misfit because what is every woman's "fulfillment" does not quiet her restlessness. Or she will suspect that it is because her children refuse to be model children that she cannot be a model mother. The wickedest wish a romantic mother can have may flash through her mind. She may wish just for once that she could be free of them. Although every little girl knows the story of Snow White, few know in advance the hard realities of motherhood.

This very predicament has been a source of fury for women who have abdicated romantic motherhood and sought some form of liberation. They think motherhood is oppressive. The noted feminist author Simone de Beauvoir argues that confining women to motherhood makes them second class. Woman's inferiority, she says, ''originated in her being at first limited to repeating life, whereas man invented reasons for living more essential, in his eyes, than the not-willed routine of mere existence.''[2]

Is It Necessary to Renounce Motherhood? Some ardent feminists believe that the only way to avoid the oppression of romantic motherhood is by not becoming a mother at all. Other women flatly deny that there are any hazards and determine to become romantic mothers even if it kills them. Well, it may, but not in the manner they may think. These are two extremes, and fortunately they are both exceptions. Today, after the era of liberation, there is still a throng of women who choose to have children because they believe that motherhood can be a fine part of life. However they also know that if it is to be fine, they will have to rethink some of the attitudes they have already formed. No matter what the relationship of mother to child is going to be, they realize that they will have to make it happen, not just let it happen.

The first few times I held my eldest child I felt as if I had done it before, almost like *déjà vu*. Yet I could not connect the memory with a past event. Maybe I only recalled my own daydreams or the times that I played mother with great intensity and anticipation. I think I am no exception. Almost every female reared in western culture has played mother at some time in her childhood or adolescence, either by tending younger children, babysitting, caring for a young animal, or playing with dolls.

No single practice session, however, forms maternal identity; our training occurs all along. Women born before the 1960s were not brought up in exactly the same way that their brothers were, although their brothers too may have tended younger children or cared for pets. What was missing for the boys were the dolls. If they did play with dolls, it was probably not more than once or twice, and not after age five. There was, however, a further important difference. Girls play nurturant roles more frequently, more publicly, and more seriously than their brothers because they take seriously the possibility of someday becoming a parent. Their brothers play only for the moment, because they are not made to be as aware as their sisters of future parenthood. This constitutes a significant difference.

Is this difference unfair to women? The ability to take care of others—to nurture—is, most assuredly, a valuable asset that few of us would like to do without. If this is true, our brothers, and not we, are the most obvious victims of sexism. If they never learned to be parental, and to care for others, then they grew up deprived. Nevertheless, we must ask how we can distinguish between the training of a valued emotional asset and a set-up for the disappointment of romantic motherhood? Three factors deserve our considereation: (1) imitation of mother, (2) doll play, and (3) the anti-motherhood myth.

Imitation of Mother. Little girls imitate their mothers as a way of confirming that they are female. The actions they choose to imitate for this purpose are the ones that distinguish mother and father. If mother and father dress quite distinctly, their daughter may imitate her mother's style of clothing; but if both parents wear pants and shirts most of the time, imitating dress will not suffice as a way for the daughter to confirm her gender. Childcare often is, but need not be, a gender cue. If both parents do their share of childcare, their daughter will imitate them both; and although she will learn parental skills, caring for little ones will not be a way of *establishing* her femaleness. The most wholesome and essential way for girls to clarify their gender is by noticing that their mothers and fathers have different bodies, and that their own bodies are more like their mother's.

Some feminists have argued that as soon as we make little girls conscious of their gender we lock them into a limited role. But neither feminists nor anyone else has demonstrated that it is parents who do this to children and not children who do this to themselves. Children seem to seek out some differences between male and female in order to assign themselves to one of these categories. They cannot wait until they are adult to discover that they are male or female. What parents can control, however, is *the basis* upon which children make their assignment to categories. Daughters learn their gender not so much by what their parents say but by what they do. Not theories, but actions demonstrate for them how their parents define their own gender. The actions are what children imitate: the girl who sees her mother doing all of the childcare while her father is excused from it may pick childcare as a gender cue; but the girl who sees her mother and father caring for children will look for some other cue for distinguishing her own gender.

That girls learn to be motherly is perfectly reasonable; that boys do not learn to be fatherly, however, is perfectly unreasonable. This mixture of reason and unreason characterizes our society. Yet we cannot correct its neglect in preparing boys to be fathers by now refusing to teach girls to be mothers. This is an important issue in the post-liberation era. Furthermore, teaching children the skills for parenthood does not obligate them to become parents. Help, protection, and caring can enrich human relationships between any two people and is not limited to parents and children.

Doll Play. Children do not play with dolls simply in order to rehearse for the future. In doll play children symbolize the present; play is a child's method of thinking things over. The affection expressed to dolls in play is often the kind children want from their own parents. Just like their dolls, they need rescue in emergencies, care when sick, defense against bullies, and attention at outings. The child who is too young to deliberate about how to interact with parents may play about it, just as an adult might daydream. Before parents decide that dolls are sexist and take them away from their daughters, they would do well to consider what an important contribution doll play can make to a child's emotional life.

Boys are seldom allowed to play with dolls; they are given stuffed animals instead. Furthermore, even the stuffed animal is "outgrown" as soon as possible. Because of this pattern, boys are directed toward play that minimizes the component of interpersonal relations and emotional expression. Is it coincidence, then, that grown men in our society find it embarrassing to talk about sensitive feelings or to admit their own needs for care and affection? Perhaps their inhibitions are not unrelated to the fact that as boys they were not allowed to play out these feelings using dolls and other toys as props.

It is only in the last decade that public consciousness is once again allowing men to be more open with their emotions and is forgiving them if they are not heroes all the time. But liberation has not yet worked through our dealings with children. In this post-liberation era we now dare to give electric trains to girls, but we are still squeamish about giving dolls to boys for fear of raising a generation of sissies. This is just one more instance of the difference between talking liberated and being liberated.

The Anti-Motherhood Myth. Once upon a time some women may have thought that motherhood was all their dreams come true, but for a decade or so the motherhood myth has been getting trimmed down to size. A vivid example is Betty Rollin's article, "Motherhood: Who Needs It?" In this article she suggests that most adolescent girls know enough about motherhood "to qualify for a master's degree."[3] When girls grow up, family, friends, and everyone else puts pressure on them to use their motherhood training. If that is not enough, Rollin adds, women themselves want babies so that they will have something to do and something to be. Children provide both a job and an identity for these women. In fact, "Motherhood offers an instant identity . . . Some women consider birth the biggest accomplishment of their lives, which may be interpreted as saying not much for the rest of their lives."[4]

The gist of Rollin's message is that women have a choice: they may either succumb to the mystique of motherhood or they may choose not to have children. With this simplistic either/or dilemma, however, writers like Betty Rollin have escaped the devil only to fall into the deep blue sea. Propagandized by these writers, many perfectly intelligent and supposedly enlightened young women feel slightly embarassed if motherhood attracts them as much as a career does. I would hate to count the number of times career-bound, college women have apologetically told me in private that having children someday is also very important to them. They are apologetic because they think that "liberated women" are not supposed to be interested in motherhood. They whisper their intentions as if they were admitting a defect. Thanks to some simple-minded reactionary thinking we have now replaced the motherhood myth with the anti-motherhood myth. What kind of progress is that?

Whether or not they eventually become mothers, it is neither unfortunate nor unfair that girls go through a stage of predisposition for motherhood. It is unfortunate, however, if motherhood is the only thing for which they are predisposed. Motherhood should not eclipse preparation for professions, responsible citizenship, social action, and other relationships. If in the past girls have been brainwashed into thinking that motherhood was the only task they were capable of doing, they must not now overreact. The solution is not to stop teaching them how to be motherly, but rather to start teaching them how to do more than just that.

In terms of motherhood, our thinking has a long way to go before it will reach a position of balanced common sense that will give girls an open and flexible future. Meanwhile, it is not likely that women who wish to have children will refrain from doing so. It is only unfortunate that they will do so with some unnecessary mixed feelings. Better preparation can help. The stage of changing predispositions for marriage and motherhood is the foundation for many other changes in women's lives.

Becoming an adult requires that we learn to scrutinize what others expect of us; but more important is this: if we are to become mature, we must be aware of our own motives and our own expectations. To evaluate these expectations means to take charge of our predispositions and our reasons for action. It also involves the realization that although we may not be able to change all the expectations that others have for us, we can choose whether we want to or ought to live up to these expectations. As we do that, we become responsible for ourselves.

5

Immersion:
Getting Involved

"... go!"

If we are to be happy we must be invested in life. Our activities must take up our energies—and give us back energy—and be worthwhile for us. A major source of vitality comes from the relationships we form. We live into them, and they form us. In some sense we are like actors on a stage. By learning to play our roles well we do more than just pretend: we invite something within us to be expressed, we actually live into the roles we play. In another sense, of course, we are not like actors at all. We cannot shed costumes, drop the expressions, and leave the part behind us. When we engage in the role we own the costume, we live the expression, we are the part. When we invest ourselves in a new segment of life we enter an immersion stage, and in terms of our personal happiness, this kind of immersion is both necessary and risky. The excitement this immersion promises compels us to invest, but the risk is that once we do we will never be the same again.

Immersion means that we leave ourselves open to influence, and allow ourselves to change. The risk involved, however, should not scare us into avoiding immersion; rather, it should challenge us to seek out the sources that influence us. Mature women do not let social convention push them into roles, nor do they let fear hold them back from living out their roles to the fullest. Fortunately, we do not have to structure our lives according to one theme and in one big maneuver. If we are wise we immerse oursleves in various themes during our lives. If we are sensitive to the pattern of our lives we will keenly sense our own readiness for a change of direction and the new surge of intensity that comes along with such a change. In adulthood we can go through numerous immersion stages in a succession of relationships. As long as we do, we can remain lively and happy.

Familiar Immersions

Women who are overly prepared for the roles of wife and mother often fail to see the variation and refreshment that a succession of relationships can provide. Because the immersion stages—the establishment—of the relationships to their husband and children are important and time consuming, they have trouble looking beyond them. When immersion in marriage and motherhood is through, however, these roles eventually take their places among other roles and leave room for development outside of them. Marriage and motherhood monopolize life only when immersion gets stuck. Let us consider each of these important immersion stages in turn.

Immersion in Marriage

The most intense stage of marriage is the stage during which husband and wife get acquainted with one another. Immersed in the relationship, they are together as much as possible, and they talk a great deal. Newlywed couples tend to do everything together—shopping, cooking, cleaning, walking the dog—and explore each other's ideas and opinions about everything. In this way they become familiar with one another. Sometimes the glee of being able to share events, thoughts, and opinions creates a sort of love-drunkenness—a revelling in being so much together, so close, and so contented. Discovering similarities of opinion, feelings, values, dreams, and perceptions strengthens a couple's sense of companionship.

Newly married couples believe their marriage is different from most other marriages; that theirs will succeed where others fail. Thus they wish that they could ignore whatever does not enhance their close and happy involvement with each other. They ignore their awkward differences, and find reassurance in their deliberate similarity.

During immersion a couple is busy making assessments of what is and what is not possible in their relationship. They discover the strengths and benefits of their partnership, but they also discover its weaknesses and disadvantages. For this reason, immersion tends to be a stage of extremes. It can be very good or very bad, but seldom is it neutral. Much of the emotional work of marriage during this stage centers on testing commitment. Healthy commitment does not spring automatically out of infatuation, but requires diligent work. One of the most difficult challenges of marriage is to find the best mix of independence and attachment. Ethicist Lewis Smedes suggests that in order to be loyal to each other, marriage partners need to be independent:

> Total self-giving, generous as it may seem, is destructive of marriage because it saps a partner of the creative independence he/she needs in order to contribute himself/herself to the other person . . . The condition for self-giving is self-assertion; every partner has a duty of fidelity to himself/herself and, equally, a duty of fidelity to let the other be a real self.[1]

Fidelity to a marriage partner and fidelity to one's self come to expression through two recurring themes in marriage: communication and power. Let's take a close look at these themes.

New Communication Habits in Marriage. How does a woman teach her husband who she is, and how does she learn who he is? How does a husband teach his wife about himself, and how does he learn about her? In the close arrangement of marriage, partners are continually exchanging messages that convey their images of themselves and their images of each other. Therefore they must seek the most effective teaching and learning method: they must ask how partners can teach each other about themselves in ways that enrich their relationship, and how they can avoid destructive communication habits.

The channels of communication are complex. Only a small fraction of the total immersion is transmitted by words. Actions, emotional expressions, and gestures are statements that we make about ourselves, and which others interpret and fit into their impressions of us. An acquaintance of mine once told me that she no longer told her husband anything that displeased her about their family because, when she did, he looked like a kicked dog. Although he never said so in words, the expression on his face clearly said she should not complain. I thought she was being unreasonable until on one occasion, when I was with them both, she said something negative and I witnessed for myself the kicked-dog expression it evoked. Everything in her husband's demeanor said that her remark made him feel awful, and that she should never say such a thing again.

Even the most verbal and self-aware person would have difficulty being understood if words were the only means of communication. The perceptions that marriage partners form of each other are an ongoing jumble of impressions tossed back and forth between them. With each additional impression, their perceptions become more complex. Our self-concepts and perceptions are seldom on a single level. As we add to, modify, distort, and echo our impressions with dizzying rapidity, it is very soon no longer clear who thinks what.

Consider for a moment what happens when marriage partners begin the process of teaching and learning about each other. Among the wife's ideas about herself is at least this simple set:

> This is what I am.
> This is what I wish I were.
> This is what I want others to think of me.

As soon as her husband becomes an important person for her, she begins to care about his opinion of her. Consequently, she adds to her set of ideas about herself:

> This is what he thinks I am.
> This is what he wishes I were.
> This is what he wants me to think he thinks of me.

In the process of getting acquainted, the wife also forms impressions of her husband both in terms of what she thinks of him and of what she thinks he thinks of himself:

> This is what I think he is.
> This is what I wish he were.
> This is what I want him to believe that I think of him.
> This is what he thinks he is.
> This is what he wishes he were.
> This is what he wants me to think of him.

Already the original illustration has expanded to a dozen statements! In real life, however, the number of statements is virtually infinite. Furthermore, the "what" of each statement is continually changing as new experiences modify impressions.

Elaborated in this fashion, the communicative network appears to be hopelessly complex. In theory, it seems futile to even begin the process of acquaintance, yet spouses do begin. In some cases they succeed in knowing each other quite well, and in other cases they seem to misperceive each other abysmally. Why the difference? Certain habits of communication strongly influence the effectiveness of communication.

Self-Statements. The first communications about ourselves must come from *us*. In a new relationship *we* need to teach the other who we are; we should not expect to know who we are from the other's expectations. Although husbands and wives do influence each other's beliefs about themselves, this influence is only healthy if it occurs after each has successfully presented her or himself to the other.

When a woman teaches—not learns from—her husband about herself, she should try to convey to him how she understands herself without sacrificing honesty for the sake of pleasing him. In turn, he can try to see *her* world—at least for the moment—through *her* eyes. In terms of communication in marriage, there is no statement more rewarding than for one partner to be told by the other, "I think I know what it is like to be you." Similarly, it is terribly disappointing to sense that your partner has heard but not really comprehended what you have said. Implicit in that experience is the message that what you think is important is actually not very important at all, and that your perceptions of yourself are, in fact, not accurate.

It is for this reason that the quarrelsome preface, "You know what you are? You're a . . ." cuts so deeply. This language says in effect that the other has no interest in what you think of yourself, and that you should replace your opinion with someone else's hostile one. The inability for husband and wife to hear what the other says is not, however, limited to quarrels. Sometimes persons who care about us refuse to take seriously what we say about ourselves because they want us to think more highly of ourselves than we do. For example, Sherry says to her husband, "I feel like a blimp; I hate being fat. I wish just for once in my life I could be thin. I've got to go on a diet." His well-meaning response is, "You shouldn't worry about your weight. You look fine. I like the way you look." But instead of feeling grateful to her husband for his reassurances, Sherry feels instead that no one in the world understands how terrible she feels about being fat. His approval does not change her opinion because he does not understand how she feels.

Couples must be active in communication from the very beginning of their relationship. Young people planning for marriage should be taught the difference between fitting into a blind marriage and *forming* a marriage in which two specific persons can live happily. Imagine the healthy effect for a man and woman planning marriage if they would deliberately formulate statements about themselves for each other. For example, she might say, "John, I'm a person who needs time to be alone without interruptions, and sometimes I will prefer being alone to being with you or anyone else. I need to have friends, and I do not plan to give them up just because I'm getting married. I am not very sure of myself sexually, and I don't want to pretend that I'm an expert." When the husband has heard his wife's statements about herself, he can make his own about himself. When both have heard the other's statements, and when both are content to let the other's statements stand without disclaimers or modification, they can be confident that they have accomplished a valuable first step in communication. Any couple not able to do this may not be acquainted well enough or communicating smoothly enough to put together a sound marriage.

Many women are inclined to default in marital communications. They are eager to be exactly the wives their husbands want, and they expect that their husbands will allow them to be ideal wives. As a consequence, marriage partners live with a double self-image that can never be brought into focus. A woman who is eager to please may try for a long time to live by the image of herself that has been derived totally from others. Her attitude is: "Just tell me what to be and I'll be it. I aim to please." Nevertheless, another self that does not perfectly fit the bill is always lingering in the shadows. Playing this game makes her childish and discontented.

Modifications. There must always be room in marriage for each of us to have an honest view of ourselves as we are as well as a hopeful image of the person we wish to become. The discrepancy between the two, if we can be open about it, is a helpful motivation to change. This same discrepancy when kept secret is unhealthy. If we are dishonest with ourselves and pretend that we are already the ideal we wish to become, it even becomes difficult for others to be candid with us. When we block communication lines in this way we invite trouble. Honesty in marital communications is essential, because only when partners trust that each is open and above board can they refrain from making final judgments.

It is hard for lovers to refrain from making final judgments about each other. They delight in making professions that last forever: "I will always love you." "Be mine always." But experience often shows that it is far wiser to hold a partner to a commitment to honesty than to exuberant and idealistic promises made in the warm glow of infatuation.

Women who are afraid to change even such things as their own opinions or feelings blame themselves when their dreams are not fulfilled. They believe that if they really love their husbands they will be happy no matter what. They do not realize that, in part, loyalty in marriage requires the courage to make a situation in which it is possible for husband and wife to love each other. Instead of working to make their lives liveable, passive women chide themselves for not being as happy as other women. This circle of despair and self-accusation is lonely. Just as once these women did not take the initiative to acquaint their husbands with themselves and their dreams, so now they hide their unhappiness about life having gone stale. Because these women sell out an honest marriage for the pretense of an ideal one, they are left with a seashell of a marriage—prettily colored on the outside but hollow within.

These women are haunted by depression; they feel hopeless and eventually they despair. They feel that they have no control over their own fates. Because they have relinquished their future, their lives promise only dreary repetition. All they can do is inwardly (and perhaps unconsciously) sigh, "This is all there will be forever . . ." Even if their depression is unfocused, however, it is not unfounded.

Learning to Balance Power in Marriage

Women who have been hurt in the emotional politics of marriage often portray men as oppressors who subjugate unwilling women to a master-slave arrangement. Yet it must be remembered that the power balance of marriage is formed from two sides. Both male domination and female default turn husband and wife into political rivals. We need only to consider the manipulation implicit in the advice of Marabel Morgan, author of *The Total Woman*. She instructs wives to deny themselves in order to accomodate their husbands—no matter what:

> I have been asked if this process of adapting places a woman on a master-slave basis with her husband. A Total Woman is not a slave. She graciously chooses to adapt to her husband's way, even though at times she desperately may not want to. He in turn will gratefully respond by trying to make it up to her and grant her desires. He may even spoil her with goodies.[2]

Some women invite this silly manipulation because they think it is a virtue. The truly sacrificing wife, however, is a great rarity; and what is called subservence most often is the use of devious means instead of a straightforward approach. The shrewd gambles of the "total women" corrupt marital power and rob women of emotional integrity. Believing they must be nice at all costs, those women usually associate niceness with weakness, and in so doing feed the problems of feminine passivity.

A woman with intentions and strength enough to have an impact on events has no reason to feel guilty. If she accepts the myth of feminine passivity, however, she is likely to fear that any personal strength is in conflict with her femininity. The battle is within her; she is not on the battlefield, but is herself the battlefield. Her worst encumbrance in the war is the guilt she feels for having a will of her own. If she finds that her own strong opinions are unwomanly, she will also find any form of power repugnant. She even feels guilty if her actions have consequences for her husband. To salve her guilt, she lets him act for both of them whenever possible.

Marriage is often a way of being active and passive at the same time. When a woman is joined by a man who acts deliberately and has a strong will, she imagines that her own need for power is satisfied through being paired with him. But this substitute for her own activity, for assuming responsibility, suffices only as long as she is so closely agreed with her husband that his actions express her wishes. The moment their wills differ and his actions counter her wishes, her passivity will begin to undermine their marriage.

Once a marriage has been established, it is difficult to change the balance of power. If the wife has already relinquished her own domain of control, gaining it back may cause hard feelings. In fact, her efforts may seem to be a gesture of distrust, because she is repossessing something she has already entrusted to her husband as an idealistic gesture of loyalty. Yet she must work to gain back some constructive power if she wants their marriage to survive. She cannot remain untouched by the politics of marriage forever. If she has tried to disengage herself from the exercise of her own will, sooner or later she will become resentful. Furthermore, she will use her passivity to reproach her husband as he blunders along in his masculine pride. Although initially she may have let him have his way because she respected him, later she will let him have his way because she respects him no longer and cannot be bothered to fight about anything. By inviting her husband to be a tyrant, a wife encourages estrangement. The relationship breaks down, and the husband and wife become opponents with no possibility for coalition.

His, Hers, and Theirs. Not only must marriage partners learn to balance power in their common life together, but they must also learn what their common life is. Too often a declaration of love removes all boundaries between each person: everything is open, shared, common. This exaggerated merger breaks down the smooth working of marital power because the identities of the two persons become unclear. What is needed is a clear understanding that there is "her" domain, "his" domain, and "their" domain.

Some couples feel that holding back anything in marriage is disloyal: every opinion, every decision, every activity must come about by common agreement. What happens in this situation, however, is that every opinion and decision is controlled by the partner who is better at commanding the lead, making a point, or stating a case. This is not even to say that the most powerful partner is self-interested or unfair. In fact, very often the process is full of good intentions. No matter how altruistically the process is directed, if one partner is always the leader and the other always the follower, the power balance of marriage becomes unhealthy.

The fairest way to decide who should take the lead in making decisions is by considering for whom the decision will have the most consequences. When the politics of marriage are worked out in this way it makes little difference who has the strongest personality, the quickest tongue, the keenest logic, or—above all—the most stubborn will. In matters that pertain primarily to her own life and activities, a woman must take the lead, be responsible, and make decisions. Similarly, in many matters the husband must be responsible to and for himself. Above all, the shared domain must in fact *be* shared, so that there is no silent party to any decision. For example, a decision is not shared when a husband says to his wife, "The job opportunities here are pretty sparse. If I'm ever going to advance I'm going to have to be somewhere with a different job market. Let's move! I think I'll apply for some jobs, put out some feelers, and see what happens." He has declared his intention. If she says nothing, both may be tempted to assume that they have made a decision together; but they will discover as they live out the consequences of their decision that their power arrangement is dangerously out of balance.

Marriages will always involve the exercise of power; about this we have no choice. However, we do have options as to the kind of power that will be exercised. When husband and wife recognize that power must be handled in marriage, they can choose between more and less wholesome forms of power. Rollo May in his book *Power and Innocence* distinguishes types of power. Exploitive power, he says, uses its victim; manipulative power is power over someone else; and competitive power is used against another person. To these he adds nutrient power, which is "for the other"; and integrative power, which is "power with the other person." These two types of power are consonant with love. He explains,

> The boundaries of power and love overlap each other. Love makes the person who loves want to be influenced and want to do what the loved one wishes. The intertwining of love and power is shown in relationships between lovers and between husband and wife in the concern for the dignity of the other, the preservation of his or her independent self.[3]

Even so, it must be realized that no matter how well-balanced the exercise of power is in marriage, no matter how clearly understood the shared and personal domains, sooner or later there will be conflict. Conflict itself is not a fatal defect; what matters more is whether or not a husband and wife can face conflict head-on and come out intact. Out of conflict comes hurt, but hurt is seldom the result of objective differences of opinion. The hurt that grows out of conflict arises from the feeling of having been judged unjustly or cheated.

It has often been said that men have short memories, but women are poor losers and hold a grudge. Although it is overstated, there is some truth to this claim. Conflict is a temporary irritation to a man, but it is a deep humiliation to a woman. No matter how just and egalitarian a husband and wife try to be, under the stress of conflict they are reminded that his rights and independence, backed by society and tradition, can be assumed. The warrior is a man, and when he fights he rises to his glory. But a woman's rights and independence are granted, for it is well nigh impossible to be an independent married woman without a husband who cooperates.

When a woman does battle she is forced to take up the weapons that society first of all offers to men. Furthermore, she must be able to bear assaults on her womanhood for she knows that in the eyes of all—and maybe even in her own—a fighting man is a hero but a fighting woman is a joke. If a woman struggles valiantly, she may be reminded that she is "just a woman." Whether she interprets that to mean, "You do not know your place," "You do not think clearly," or "You wish you were a man," she feels the rebuke. Then even if she wins her point, she feels her victory as a humiliation.

Sensing the difficulties, many women refuse to contend wholeheartedly with their husbands. The wife gives in to her husband's will with silent resentment, and thus finds only partial comfort. She never really wins, and she never really loses. She just gives up. In the place of conflict, which is not fatal to marriage, she offers an indifference that is sure to kill. This indifference, unfortunately, is a passive woman's most ready and familiar weapon.

Stalemates. A while ago, I was listening to a radio talk show as I was driving home. The topic was about who makes the final decision when husband and wife have argued and argued and still cannot agree. Listeners, mostly women, called in to tell their stories. One woman told how she and her husband had quarreled because he wanted a new fishing boat and she wanted a frost-free refrigerator. She persisted, and won. But all summer long, every

Saturday that it did not rain, she felt guilty that her husband was not out fishing. She began to wish the victory had not been hers. Callers piled one story on another, giving examples of conflicts that came to some arbitrary solution. It seemed that one partner always gave in, the other walked off with the spoils, and neither was happy.

Why did they give in? Several women cited the old rule that says if husband and wife have talked out a disagreement as much as they can and they still cannot agree, then the husband should exercise his prerogative as head of the household and make the final decision. Other women suggested that they gave in because they believed that they would bruise their husbands' egos too badly if they continued the quarrel too long.

Marriages cannot endure many arbitrary decisions of this kind. Such decisions encourage a tyranny that makes one person ugly and the other powerless. Furthermore, such solutions are unnecessary. They are based on the false assumption that marriage is a closed system with which no one else should interfere. Husbands and wives do not have to make decisions as if they are a jury sequestered from the public until the verdict is spoken. When husband and wife cannot agree, the obvious solution is to call in a third party to help them.

When husbands and wives are alone they will argue with each other in a manner that they would not consider if a third person were present. The difference is not just a matter of face-saving. Rather, the difference is created by the fact that the third person does not have an investment in the outcome, and is not hearing the argument within the context of past conflicts, unresolved grudges, or tests of affection. Often the peacemaker can have a settling influence simply by letting husband and wife each present their case. Moreover, the possibility of calling in a third person to soothe conflict relieves the claustrophobia of marital conflict. It cuts the tightness of a situation where two pesons are locked in ruthless conflict with the attitude that one must win and the other lose.

There is a catch to calling in a third person, however. The tough question is, who are you going to ask? What will happen if the husband wants to invite his friend and the wife wants to invite hers? Here is another instance in which planning beforehand proves invaluable. We arrange godparents for children, why not arrange guardians for marriage? Before a couple is ever caught in stalemate they could very well decide whom they could both trust for outside help. For obvious reasons, they would be wise to avoid members of either's family. In fact, establishing a marriage guardian might even be a wise and meaningful addition to the marriage ceremony. Not only would this be a practical move, it would also be a helpful reminder to bride and groom that marriage is not meant to fence them off from the world and leave them at each other's mercy.

Immersion in Motherhood

Why is motherhood so often viewed in the extremes of total sacrifice or cruel indifference? The madonna or the wicked stepmother? There is an unfair tendency to view motherhood as a mother's masterpiece, while in reality it is a partnership between mother and child. It is the fortunate mother who can break through these misconceptions and develop the attitude that she and her child are in a venture together, and if it is to work they must each do their part.

Many mothers have been brainwashed into believing that any effort on the part of a mother to care for herself is contrary to motherhood. Her interests, so the myth goes, are contrary to her children's interests. Therefore she must sacrifice herself for the sake of the species. If she is unhappy it is definitely because she is a bad mother; if she is happy because she has done something for her own happiness, she may also be considered a bad mother. There is a peculiar suspicion of happy mothers, as if their happiness is a sure sign that they are selfish—and selfishness is a mother's greatest sin. Immersion in motherhood presents a double bind for women who buy wholeheartedly into the motherhood myth.

Some respected authorities on the psychology of women have propagated this self-destructive notion among women. For example, Helene Deutsch in the *Psychology of Women* says of motherhood:

> We find in it a world of polarities—ego interests and service to the species, the mother's tendency to preserve her unity with the child and the child's drive to freedom, love, and hostility, and a large number of personal, frequently neurotic conflicts.[4]

It's no wonder that motherhood is intimidating! Women are encouraged to approach it with a perfectionism that gives rise to guilt and self-recrimination for every shortcoming. Anything less than a perfect child is testimony to the mother's inadequate skills. As a consequence many women begin motherhood already defeated, for they fear that every personal flaw will be magnified by motherhood and objectified in the victim-child.

We have had enough of this talk about service to the species. It is time we ask what there is in motherhood for mothers. This is not a popular question, but it needs to be asked. First of all, we must ask it because mothers themselves do not experience motherhood only as a service for the good of society or the species or even their own children. They experience it also as a relationship that is pleasurable and rewarding. Mothers can and do benefit from motherhood, and if given the choice to live their lives again, few women with children would choose to omit this part of their lives. Let's take a look at two of the benefits of motherhood, intimacy and receptivity.

Intimacy. One of the benefits of being a parent is the possibility of affectionate intimacy with children. Few people know us as well as our children do; in fact, there is not much of significance about us that our children do not know. This is true even for things we never talk about. The closeness experienced between a mother and her children gives rise to strong feelings, both good and bad. These are the emotions of intimacy. Toward those with whom we are intimate we can feel swelling and mellow affection. For example, with our children we can sit side by side, nestled close together reading a story book or watching television, and in this simple moment feel the purest peace and contentment. We can also feel the most biting disappointment and anger toward those with whom we are intimate. Sometimes children test their parents with cruelty, defiance, or hostility. These are the risks of intimacy.

Intimacy and risk go together because in closeness there is always the danger of self-loss. A mother's fear of the dependence of her children is not a symptom of an unhealthy relationship; more likely it is the symptom of a healthy one. Perhaps this dream illustrates the fear:

> I dreamed I was nursing a baby. As the baby sucked it kept getting larger and larger, and I kept getting smaller and smaller. Finally I saw

in the dream a monstrous child sucking its fist. Although I was still observing everything, it was as if I didn't really exist anymore.

When Helene Deutsch suggests that there is a conflict between the interests of the child and the mother—mother wants to hold on while child wants to let go, mother is other-serving while child is self-serving—she misses an important point. There are two well-balanced tendencies within the mother herself, and if she learns to respect these, they will keep her attachment to her children healthy. The one tendency tells the mother that she must preserve herself, that she must not let her children use her up. It allows her to sense the maternal dignity in sometimes saying "no" to a child.

The first time a mother leaves her newborn in someone else's care she is saying to the child, "You cannot be with me constantly because we are distinct." The mother who allows herself this experience of distinctness often experiences a fresh surge of love for her child when she returns to it again. When a mother refuses to be interrupted by an impatient child she is saying, "No, you cannot have my attention whenever you please." Once the mother tries out her "no" and finds she can make it work, she also finds in herself a new eagerness to give rewarding attention.

When a mother says "no" on these occasions she is doing more than providing good discipline so that her child will not grow up dependent, rude, and devious. Mothers say "no" for their own sakes as well. Their dignity is worth preserving, their freedom has merit, and their persons deserve consideration. Moreover, the ability to say "no" to children seems to support the mother's freedom to love her children. This is what happens when the mother leaves her infant for the first time. She tests the elasticity of the relationship, and she finds that she can move close or have some distance. Both she and the child benefit from this flexibility, because it makes affection a choice rather than an obligation. Without it, attachment easily degenerates into duty, and the loss of freedom steals the joy of caring for children.

The dream about the devouring baby is a sign that the mother needs some distance from her child in order to deal with her own fear. Fear—or perhaps awe—always lurks in the shadows as we experience things that are intensely important to us. We feel awe when we realize that our happiness in every relationship rests on a "what if." What if we should lose what we treasure? What if we love and are not loved back? These fears surface not when we have doubts about close relationships, but when we are most invested in them. The same mother who had the dream about the devouring baby eventually learned to take a distance from her children when she needed it, and later she writes:

> Sometimes when I look at my children I love them so much I could burst, or weep, or just squeeze them with delight. Sometimes I sigh quietly with an intense joy. Then, in this, I feel close to my instincts, and I think I know something about the kind of being I am. As a liberated woman I should know better than to be caught up by such an old-fashioned passion? I will not give in to the pressures of time that would take this away for the sake of freedom. Why should I destroy my own happiness?

Receptivity. Just as we see good motherhood as self-protective, we can also recognize motherhood as important to mothers because of what their children give to them. This too requires breaking with some long-held ideas that have formed our expectations. It is startling that even so respected a psychologist as Erich Fromm can suggest:

> For most children before the age of eight and a half to ten, the problem is almost exclusively that of *being loved*—of being loved for what one is. The child up to this age does not yet love; he responds gratefully, joyfully to being loved.[5]

Such a view creates a conflict in maternal feelings, because it suggests that mothers only imagine that their children love them. Furthermore, it seriously devalues the quality of a child's love, and belittles the rich mother-child love relationship.

We cannot, however, automatically assume that a mother feels the love of her child. There are some important prerequisites for being open to a child's love. First, in order to accept a child's affection a mother needs confidence and self-worth. It is tragic when a woman hungers after the love of a child because she has never felt loved by anyone else. Sadly, she will not even be able to accept a child's love unless she believes that she is lovable. Furthermore, she must believe that she is lovable even when her child does not love her.

Children need to give their love freely; they must also be free not to give it. This realization is a second prerequisite for a mother being open to a child's love. If expressions of affection are to be honest they must not be coerced, nor must anger, rejection, or distance be stifled. The love a child expresses is not just a mirror image of its mother's attachment and affection. If it were, the child would only be a prop in a narcissistic circle, and the mother's own love reflected back to herself would only be a form of self-love. Children have their own centers of emotion and affection, and the love they give is a gift.

The third prerequisite for receiving a child's love is the realization that love is not a limited quantity. A child's affection for someone else will not get in the way of its love for its mother. Exclusive love easily becomes destructive. The mother who believes that whatever affection goes to someone else is affection that she will not get turns the child's spontaneous loving feelings into obligation. Instead of affection the child feels guilt, and instead of giving its mother an emotional gift, the child only carries out a duty.

Perhaps this all sounds very idealistic, but it is real and not so very complex. We need only look at some examples to see that this is so. One of the most significant gifts children give to their mothers is the possibility of taking part in a child's world. Many adults look back to childhood with a nostalgia that is both sweet and painful with things remembered. Although the parent can never truly be a child again, it is possible through one's own children to be a happy guest in their world. Children are masters of play, laughter, drama, and the sport of making routine occurences into ceremonial events. In this they are our teachers.

If we let them, children will teach us to be honest with our emotions. To share tears of hurt and frustration, to laugh at themselves for being silly, or to delight in a surprise is natural for children. Mothers easily underestimate how understanding children can be, and how keenly aware they are of what goes on in their parents' lives. A rather touching example of this appears in Violet Weingarten's *A Woman of Feeling*. A woman is called to testify against the members of a political organization with which she has worked. She is torn apart by the conflict between legal pressure and loyalty to her co-workers. Many years later, in recollecting the event with her daughter, the mother recounts how sensitively her daughter understood the struggle going on in her mother's conscience:

Well, that night I went into your room to kiss you goodnight, and I found you staring at the ceiling, and do you know what you said to me? "I've been thinking, Mommie. It's like when the teacher goes out of the room and the kids hack around, and she comes back and asks who did it. You can't tell on them, can you? She shouldn't expect you to, should she? It's not fair."[6]

The mother goes on to recollect how just before leaving for school the next morning the young daughter had given her mother a book with the instruction that she should read it on the train. The book was *Charlotte's Web*, and:

When she opened the book, dutifully waiting until the sleeper started, a half-sheet of folded lined paper fell out. "To Mom," it said on the outside, "Dear Mom," Maggie had written carefully, "This is my *faverot* book. Please think of me as you read it. Very much love. Maggie.[7]

Children are more than charges, they are partners in an important part of our lives. Just as mothers take interest in the lives of their children, so also children participate in the lives of their mothers. Where the interests are balanced, both thrive.

New Forms of Immersion

Once the most conventional relationships—marriage and motherhood—are established, what is there left to do? When immersion in these relationships moves along in a healthy manner, they require less energy. Attention then can eventually be directed to sources beyond these relationships. In fact, to stay healthy we need new forms of immersion. Because this is true, friendship and work are two important forms of potential immersion that merit our consideration.

Immersion in Friendship

Although the value of friendship seems obvious enough, it is peculiarly absent from the lives of many people. A powerful, unspoken expectation seems to leave many believing that significant human relationships can only occur within the family. Unfortunately, this mentality not only stifles life outside of the family, it also demands that the family meet all the needs of each member.

Such expectations are unrealistic. A wife and mother who shoulders much of the responsibility for her family's well-being, has to have objects of interest outside the family, for the sake of her own well-being. Unfortunately, many women believe that their husbands and children should be able to fill all their needs for love, affection, understanding, encouragement, companionship, security, and happiness.

Women have not always been as isolated in the family as they are today. In the past, women belonged to what seemed to be natural groups and were together on a daily basis. Married, single, old, or young, the women helped make up a group in what was known as an extended household. In this situation, women had a valuable line of continuity in education for life. The more experienced taught the less experienced, who did the same for the next generation.

The contemporary woman faces a double problem. On the one hand she is part of a generation in which the skills of friendship have fallen into disuse, on the other hand, with modern life in rapid flux, she needs the security of friendship. Because the roles of women in society are less structured than before, each woman can choose from an immense range of possibilities what kind of woman she wants to be. These decisions cannot, however, be properly made without comradeship, advice, and the wisdom of shared experience. Women in the liberation gap need friends. If they sense this need, they will find new ways of protecting friendship; if they do not, they will suffer severely in their loneliness.

Friendship is a difficult relationship to describe, much more difficult than that of a parent, child, spouse, or sibling. For one thing, friendship lacks the institutionalized, public forms that define other relationships so clearly. It has no legal forms, it is not recorded, and it is issued no certificate for documentation. Furthermore, society does little to promote a set of values for friendship. No ceremonial event signals the beginning of a friendship, and condolences are not offered when a friend is lost. Friendship is not celebrated today, nor even assumed.

The meaning of friendship is so unclear that the very term has become blurred. What does it mean when we identify someone as a friend? One who is called a friend may be anything from a colleague with whom one eats lunch to a fellow rider in a car pool. Even neighbors who get together twice each year for a picnic may be considered friends because the dinstinction between a friend and an acquaintance is hardly recognized. I am reminded here of the exuberant college freshman who told me she just loved college because she had already made dozens of new friends—and after only six weeks of school.

In English, it is nearly an insult to call someone an acquaintance. This is not, however, true of other languages. In many, the distinction between friends and acquaintances is indicated by the way in which you speak to them. For example, the French language has two forms of the word "you." When speaking to a close friend or relative, the informal form of the word is used; when speaking more formally an entirely different form is used. In contrast, Americans promote the address of people by their first name and in familiar terms, no matter to whom they are talking. In such a system, everyone who is not your enemy passes as a friend. As prevalent as such a loose definition is, however, we need to be more specific for our discussion.

Who is a friend? What is friendship? Friends like each other, and their liking grows into hearty attachment. With this attachment comes the most important quality of friendship—loyalty. Friends count on each other, and they try not to let each other down. Although initially they may be drawn to each other because of common interest, loyal friends can accept differences without question. They do not idealize each other, nor do they need to change each other; their loyalty rests on an unforced readiness to accept one another as they are.

Unconditional acceptance, one of the hallmarks of friendship, is a difficult notion for many people. Fearing that unconditional acceptance necessitates the approval of faults, they do not see this is exactly what is unnecessary when acceptance is without conditions. Acceptance no-matter-what by a friend is an invitation for us to be honest about ourselves. Still, friends do care about our faults and weaknesses. They may even wish for *our* sakes that we could be free of them, but they do not make overcoming weaknesses or correcting faults a condition for friendship. This openness evokes a response in us: when we feel truly accepted by a friend, it is hard to be dishonest with that person. What's more, when we are honest with others and they with us, it is almost impossible for us to be dishonest with ourselves.

Sometimes friendship is promoted as the holiday of human

relationships. Whereas in other relationships there are respon- sibilities and commitments, the notion goes that friendship is free. This idea actually minimizes the real value friends have for each other. Loyal friendship is not a form of sentimentality that springs up to paint a rosey glow over a gloomy picture; rather, the loyalty is built on persistent honesty. A fast friend can look at our faults without flinching or looking away for the sake of courtesy. In such instances, however, friendship can be hard work. It is easy to tolerate flaws in a friend if the flaws do not bother us personally, but sticking with a friend whose habits or traits hurt, disappoint, or frustrate us is the real test of friendship. Only a strong, loyal friend can say, "I know the worst side of you, and I'll stick with you anyway. You make me angry, but I still care about you."

Too often the people we call our friends fall short of the defini- tion, and cause us to mistrust others. Some people are around when it suits them, but are nowhere to be found when we really need their support. Others we call friends cannot handle dif- ferences of opinion, and betray us when they arise. Most of us count these pseudo-friends as true friends, and suffer needless hurt. We should heed the ancient advice concerning friends that counsels:

> A faithful friend is a sure shelter.
> Whoever finds one has found a rare treasure.
> A faithful friend is something beyond price,
> There is no measuring a true friend's worth.[8]

We need true friends, both female and male, for some very specific reasons. First, friendship helps us discover new ways to live out our gender. Male friends can help us learn different things about ourselves than female friends can, for each have ex- periences that have been determined by their own gender. Regardless of whether these different experiences are the outcome of physical-chemical factors or social training, the fact remains that men and women in our society do not have the same background or experience. How then, knowing that our experience is molded by gender, do we live productively? We deal with the influences of gender by thoroughly understanding what they are and clearly defining their limits. Friends can help us do this.

We are assuming, then, that the way in which women friends help us learn our gender is distinct from that of men friends. In both cases, however, they help us by offering us understanding that clarifies our self-consciousness. The difference is that the understanding of another woman is empathic while that of a man is vicarious. Another woman can understand certain of our experiences because they are her own. Her understanding is based on recognition. As we tell our story, she says, "I know exactly what you mean." The implication is "me too." A man, however, can only understand many events in a woman's life if he imagines his way into an experience that is not his own. Thus he bridges the gap of difference. In contrast to that of a woman, his understanding response is, "I think I can imagine what that is like." Both ways of understanding have merit, but they also have limits. Let's consider them each in turn.

Empathic Understanding. Initially we learn what womanhood means from other women, and similarly men learn what manhood means from other men. We fill in the gaps of our self-awareness by describing, questioning, and sharing common impressions with persons whose lives are like ours. There is, however, a common misunderstanding that women learn about womanhood from men. This is demonstrated by the familiar expression, "He made a woman out of her," which usually refers to some sexual initiation. The implication is that sex comprises the limits of our gender, and that our gender is primarily genital. Being a woman, however, is more complex than having a sexual relationship with a man: no woman discovers what it means to be a woman by asking a man to tell her. In terms of building a good relationship, a woman is much better off if she can teach a man about femaleness than if she expects him to teach her. But before she can teach, she must learn.

Through empathy, one woman learns from another about herself by having her words, thoughts, feelings, or expressions echoed back at her. This sensitive communication relies very little on verbal precision. Sometimes a few words, a fragment of memory, or a certain knowing glance can trigger a response of recognition. Alice Rossi calls this kind of friendship sisterhood:

> First, and very importantly, it means affinity—the natural affinity of persons who discover that they can communicate with each other implicitly, using incomplete sentences and gestures. Normally this feeling arises only after persons have been friends for a long time; and often it never does. But now many women are coming to understand how their backgrounds as women in this society have given

them reservoirs of common experience. Affinity for other women—sisterhood—follows from this understanding.[9]

This kind of awareness can further be illustrated by example. When talking with a female colleague one day, I asked, ''Do you know how it feels to be the only woman in a group of all men at work?'' She replied that she too had observed that being the only woman in a group was somehow different than being in a more evenly mixed group. When I asked her what the difference was, she told me that although she shared my feeling of mild discomfort she had not thought about it carefully enough to give it a name. Nevertheless, we both knew that we were talking about the same thing and that recognition created a certain reassurance. By our recognition we also alerted each other to watch on future occasions for what exactly makes us feel awkward in that particular situation. Our conversation produced a support system for each of us. What's more, I will never again feel as alone in a group of male co-workers—my empathic friend will be there with me.

The way I feel in a group of all-male colleagues is not likely the same as the way a man would feel if he were alone in a roomful of women colleagues. Society has trained men and women for different roles in these situations. If a man tries to understand how I feel as a woman in a group of men, he may approximate the event as closely as possible with something similar in his own experience, but at a certain point he has to jump the gap of difference. If he does that and in so doing understands me, it is because he is willing to recognize a significant way in which our experiences differ. Rather than empathic, his understanding is vicarious.

Although the example I have chosen is limited to a professional world that not all women share, the difference between empathic and vicarious understanding is apparent in any woman's world. The difference between the mother's and father's role in pregnancy and childbirth can serve equally to illustrate how gender limits empathy. No matter how involved a husband is in going through these events with his wife, there are certain elements of his wife's experience he cannot share empathically. Similarly, most women probably do not understand what it is like to become a father.

In the last stages of labor, just before the actual birth, a woman feels overwhelmed by what is happening. She knows there is no going back, no way out; she of all people cannot change her mind or leave the scene. This feeling cannot be the same for the father. Ultimately, he can separate himself from the event by a mere act of will. He can leave the room; he can think about something else; he can create whatever distance he needs. He may not choose to do this, but the mere fact that he can means that his sense of the inevitable happening is different from that of his wife's. If he understands her feeling, it is because she has described it to him and he is able to imagine what it is like. In contrast, a woman who has also given birth does not need to fill in the gap with imagination. She knows: a look, a smile, a word or two can signal this recognition of common experience.

I could give more and more such examples, but you must search your life for your own examples. It is, indeed, healthy to discover and own your gender through the mirror of empathy. Knowing, acknowledging, and admitting who and what you are is a first important step to acting as you are. Friends assist in this process of maturity.

Vicarious Understanding. Just prior to adolescence, girls and boys part ways and seldom socialize together. When socializing between the sexes resumes again, it is colored by the games of courtship and marriage. If a young woman has a male friend he is called "just a friend," which is a way of saying that he's not very important. The important male in her life is called a boyfriend, and she usually has only one. The terms for designating these relationships are not only unclear, they give these relationships a childish connotation: Why is the term "boyfriend" and not "manfriend"? Furthermore, once a woman has a "boyfriend" the men who fall into the catagory of "just a friend" are usually dropped. The only common exceptions to this are her boyfriend's buddies and her womenfriend's men. In each case, her relationship to these men is a matter of social convenience and is mediated through another person. Serious friendships that are not romances are uncommon between women and men. For this, women suffer because they need men friends in order to mature.

Empathic friendship teaches a woman how she is like other women and different from men: it helps her to own her gender. Vicarious friendship teaches a woman how she is different from men, but also like them in many ways that go beyond her gender.

Friendship with a man keeps her from being closed in or unnecessarily restricted by her gender. Vicarious understanding teaches her to deal with similarity and difference at one and the same time.

It would be unfortunate if we were to conclude that either empathic or vicarious understanding is of higher quality or of more importance than the other. The latter takes more effort, but a great compliment is paid when someone is willing to work far enough past differences to understand us. Furthermore there is much to be learned for the woman who succeeds in understanding a man's world through his eyes.

Honest friendships between men and women are important in the era of liberation. In the past there was pressure on women to devalue themselves and to hold men in high esteem. Out of reaction and in the delight of finding self-affirmation some women have now made the female experience the new standard, and they devalue men. Maleness, or any hint of the masculine stereotype offends reactionary women; to them, only that which is female is good. Replacing an old offense by a new one, however, offers little advance. If women are genuinely concerned with their own maturity, they must learn to appreciate both similarity and difference. This appreciation can best be formed in friendships with both men and women.

Androgyny. Although the human race is divided into males and females, it is not divided into "masculines" and "feminines." In every woman's personality there is a masculine side, and in every man's a feminine side. Neither the masculine component of a woman's personality nor the feminine component of a man's is alien to the person. Rather, this complexity of personality helps persons avoid being as flat as the male and female stereotypes. Slavishly feminine women and exaggeratedly masculine men, having poured their energies into their images, are pathetic and boring. In contrast, the more complex personality with an interplay of masculine and feminine has resilience, variation, and liveliness. In the words of Virginia Woolf, "In each of us two powers preside, one male, one female . . . The normal and comfortable state of being is that when the two live in harmony together, spiritually cooperating." Woolf believed that creativity originates in the person who has developed these two powers, and called such a person "androgynous." She was, morever, convinced that the "androgynous mind is resonant and porous; that it transmits emotion without impediment; that it is naturally creative, incandescent, and undivided."[10]

Far more important than debating whether specific traits are accurately labeled "masculine" or "feminine," we must see that, at least in our culture, there tends to be differences of personality along gender lines. Girls and boys, men and women, do not live in identical worlds. At the same time, the more distinctly we try to draw the lines between masculinity and femininity, the more apparent it becomes that there is some of both in all of us. From here we are led to explore which experiences are conducive to that "normal and comfortable state of being."

The feminine psyche with a harmonious masculine side grows as a woman constructs her own understanding of an androgynous world. Her first impressions of the masculine counterpart arise through vicarious experience. In a harmonious and open relationship to a man, she sees the world through his eyes and comes to realize that neither her own nor his perception is absolute, but that they complement each other. What was initially vicarious experience for a woman, what could only be experienced through someone who is different, becomes her own because it cultivates this other side of her personality. As her femininity grows new domains of awareness open up to her.

Useful vicarious experience does not occur in superficial socializing between men and women. In superficial contacts, persons have little personal knowledge of each other but depend on stereotypes. Such a dependence calls us to play a part ourselves. It is only when we take off the masks that the distinctness and complexity of persons can be seen. One means of overcoming artificiality, of taking off the masks, is by cultivating genuine friendships.

The Subversion of Friendship. If friendship has so much to offer, why is it not credited more highly? One of the worst attacks on friendship has come from the tradition of Freudian psychology. According to Sigmund Freud, our energies for attachment and affection are sexual, and we are in the best state when these energies have one object. The initial object of love is mother, and the ultimate object should be a mate. At times, according to Freudian theory, a transition person becomes the object of love between mother and mate, and that person is the adolescent friend.

In the case of girls, a friend is enough like a mother to make the substitution adequate, and enough like the girl herself to make the friend likeable. In essence, then, Freudian theory sees friendship as a normal form of homosexuality, which is relinquished in adulthood when a heterosexual mate is found.

Freud's view had enormous impact. His assertion that all affection is basically sexual is applied even by non-Freudians to all personal relationships, with the possible exception of that between parent and child. Consequently, many people feel threatened by friendship. A woman, it is assumed, may only have a man friend if she is looking for a mate; if a married woman chooses a man for a friend, she is assumed to be having an affair. Close friendships with women are also off limits because they are thought to be homosexual. In many cases this means that women not only neglect to seek friendships, but they deftly avoid them.

In convincing us that every form of intimacy is sexual, the Freudians have robbed us of a bit of childhood wisdom that we should have turned into adult common sense. As children we learned that closeness, comfort, intimacy, and attachment do not have to end in sexual union. In our families we were close to parents and grandparents, brothers and sisters, and our intimacy did not turn into blind instincts that ran away with us. If the psychoanalytic tradition insists on calling all of these intimacies—including friendship—sexual, then the term no longer has any clear meaning. Furthermore, if the term has become useless we may as well drop it, and in so doing avoid the scare associated with it.

A second reason some people avoid friendship is because it has the consequences of all close attachments, and calls us to deal with responsibility, dependence, unpredictability, and commitment. If you get close to people, they influence you and you influence them. This mutual influence is on the level of feelings, which means you cannot just turn it on and off as you can the sort of influence that is based on money or superficial charm, for example. Emotional involvement is a threat to people who make a virtue of autonomy. Understanding autonomy as a form of arbitrariness, they jealously preserve the take-it-or-leave-it attitude characteristic of shallow relationships. Such autonomy, however, has its price when taken to the extreme: it results in a closed, hidden, and boring emotional life.

The idealization of autonomy is a puzzling but popular social phenomenon. Those who prize independence supposedly do so because it allows for greater freedom and more self-direction. Sometimes the rationale given for self-sufficiency is that it allows you to do exactly what you please when you please: with no obligations to anyone, you are not held back or mired down by others. Therefore, independence becomes the new ideal and attachment to others is scorned. But people who not only enjoy but thrive on serious relationships with others recognize the idealization of such autonomy as self-destructive.

The meaning of attachment is often understood to be loss of freedom. But this is a poor understanding, because attachments only become confining if they become exclusive. For example, they are confining to persons who view their capacity for emotional investment in others as if it were the money in a Monopoly game—if you spend it all, you are out of the game. In reality, our capacity for human involvement is a nearly unlimited quantity. Only a relationship that makes demands on us with the condition "this and nothing more" is stifling. By contrast, any relationship that takes its place among the others that form our lives increases our freedom. Such relationships widen the margins of our experience by opening new possibilities, offering delights, and increasing wisdom. In this sense, attachment, commitment, and involvement in friendship to not detract from but rather increase our freedom and—paradoxically—our independence. Friendship calls forth in us the maturity and confidence that come from knowing ourselves and the world in which we live.

Immersion in Vocation

A woman, if she is to be adult and mature, must choose a vocation. Furthermore, the choice must be a real one. She must ask herself, "What shall I do, what can I do well, what can I be happy doing?" When a person becomes immersed in work, the effect is visible. Any worker needs to feel the satisfaction of being well-matched to the job, and a woman needs that as much as a man does. Her talents, then determine what job she should have. Some women find a sense of accomplishment in keeping a home and caring for children, and other women find their vocation outside the home in employment. There is, however, another group of unfortunate women who have no sense of vocation at all.

A Vocation in the Home. We feel a pang of pity for the woman who, with a sigh, identifies herself as "just a housewife." Her statement exposes the anonymity of her position. At the same time we have every reason to feel a deep respect for the woman who has the skills for a domestic vocation. If a woman is to find fulfillment, she must be in a place that is right for her. How is it that some women can find satisfaction in a domestic vocation, but others feel restless unless they are working elsewhere? We must explore this further: it is too simplistic an explanation to say that one group represents "fulfilled femininity" and the other "maladjusted discontents."

More to the point, and certainly more helpful in allowing us to respect the homemaker's vocation, is this fact: some women can and some women cannot find a sense of vocation in managing a household for their family. The degree to which a woman finds satisfaction in managing a household is, moreover, no measure of her love and devotion for her family. Rather, a woman's satisfaction with domestic tasks is related to her ability to do and enjoy this type of work. In this framework, not every woman can be a good housewife.

Many of our notions of housewifery come from the romantic ideal of the pioneer woman. Her importance is not worth disputing. The fact is, the well-being of her family depended to a large extent on her competence and skill. Even though she and her family lived far from the city or at some distance from other families, she was never isolated from the world of work. Home was the domain of work, and she did her share. Within the pioneer family, where labor was necessary for survival, her share was as essential and worthy of respect as any other.

The example of the pioneer woman is not an isolated one. Division of labor also occurred in the small-town family. The shopkeeper, tailor, baker, blacksmith, and inn-keeper carried on businesses that were extensions of the home. Beyond question, then, women were on the scene, essential partners in the family's livelihood.

The twentieth century, with its expansion of the middle class, urbanization, and centralization of work, has made these domestic vocations obsolete. The pioneer woman sharing in the tasks of taming the land and providing necessities is a lost phenomenon. Her granddaughter is the middle-class, affluent housewife whose physical survival is no struggle at all, and whose standard for what is necessary would have been her grandmother's standard for what is convenient. The wife of the townsman is no longer a business partner. Today the working man goes off to work in a place as unfamiliar to his wife as a foreign country. If she remains at home, she is not a co-worker but a co-consumer, spending with him the income he brings home after a week's work. The middle-class housewife is now called a lady, the name once reserved for a woman of the privileged class, and she manages an elaborate household. Her laundress is Whirlpool, her cook Betty Crocker. Hoover cleans her carpets, Johnsons waxes her floors, Windex shines her windows, and anything this able crew leaves undone is picked up by a "cleaning lady," the one-day-a-week help.

The maintenance of a household has shrunk in every respect. If there is a vocation for women at home, it is not housekeeping but childcare. Children, when they are young, do need a lot of attention. Assuming, then, that there are years during which a woman can make a full-time career of caring for children and maintaining a family home, let us look at what is involved in such a vocation.

The Problem of Isolation. The homemaker works alone; her vocation is not teamwork. She may drink coffee with her neighbor or chat with a friend on the telephone, but she does her work by herself. Loneliness is one of the occupational hazards of housewives. A small percentage of women who are loners may find it comfortable to be at home alone with children for eight, nine, or ten hours during the day, but many women in these circumstances desperately long for the company of another adult.

Employment outside the home has a way of creating natural social contacts. Persons who work together build natural social contacts. They are not occasional visitors; they know each other well because they are together regularly. Unlike purely social visits, work provides socializing that is natural and unselfconscious. Conversation is easy—work itself provides common topics and silence is comfortable. Furthermore, the time spent socializing over work does not seem aimless. Conversations at coffee and lunch breaks, and talk passed back and forth over work are not incidental, but rather are a rewarding social dimension of work.

Setting Limits. Another problem faced by self-employed people is that of distinguishing between work time and leisure time. People who spend all of their time working are critically labeled "workaholics." The implication is that these people should cut back, learn to relax, and stop letting their work consume their lives. Although homemakers are among some of the worst workaholics, the term is seldom used in reference to them. When asked what they do for leisure time, many women—especially mothers—are not able to answer. They take for granted that as long as they have small children, they are on call every minute of the day, and sometimes during the night as well.

To remain happy at homemaking, a woman must be able to set her own limits. She must learn to say, "I've put in a full day of work, and what is left to do will have to be done another time." This sense of one's limits also applies to childcare. For example, some mothers need time off from children, and not always for special reasons. One of the most accomplished homemakers I know has taken time out from her family by simply checking into a motel. Not only was the rest good for her, but the self-respect she demonstrated by doing this was good for her family. In a very concrete way she strengthened her family's understanding that homemaking is her vocation, and no matter how expert she is and how rewarding her vocation, she needs rest from it.

Knowing Your Own Needs. To be an accomplished homemaker requires taking the initiative to make working conditions tolerable. Homemaking is a job that requires the support of others, and to a certain extent the success of a homemaker is dependent on her ability to get this support. Unless a woman is quite skilled at being assertive, others may try to tell her what she needs. I am reminded of Carol, who after an exhausting day with a very active family and a busy pre-schooler, asked her husband if he would take over the children when he came home from work so that she could sleep. His response was that what she really needed was an evening out, and they should go out for dinner. After the children were fed and settled down for the evening, the babysitter arrived and husband and wife went out for dinner. He had arranged to meet some friends at the restaurant, and so they had a long leisurely dinner and good company. When they arrived home after midnight, Carol asked her husband if he would get up with the children so she could sleep in. His reply was, "Honestly, some people are never satisfied." She felt angry with him because he could not understand her situation; he felt angry with her because he thought that she was unappreciative. The next day he sent her flowers to patch up the quarrel. Through it all, however, Carol never got her few hours of extra sleep because she could not make clear what she knew she needed.

A slightly more positive example of self-denied needs is the homemaker who has too much to do. She must approach her family and tell them she needs to cut back on her workload. If she really intends to do that, she might ask each family member to think of some things that she does that are dispensable, she might delegate some tasks to family members, or she might warn them in advance that in the future, with no malicious intentions, she will be saying "no" to some requests.

If women are to make a satisfying vocation out of work in the home, they must develop appropriate attitudes and skills. Like other self-employed persons, they must learn how to organize time, how to set limits in work, and how to meet their own needs for work satisfaction. Women who do not do this become depressed and angry as they see their days hum-drum by, and feel used instead of appreciated.

Someone may object to all of this talk about wife-mother homemakers, and point to the fact that here and there an adventurous male is a homemaker. What is true of women is no less true of men in the same role. To derive satisfaction from homemaking, the homemaker—male or female—must make it a genuine vocation.

With a typical family size of two children, the average mother has from five to ten years during which she has children at home who require her constant attention. Once children are in school, or by the time she is about forty years old, a block of her time can be re-allocated. What will she do? Commonly, she will turn to community activities, hobbies, or employment.

Getting a Job. Returning to work or being employed for the first time is no simple matter for women who have already had a first vocation at home. The housewife in her thirties or forties going out to work has a number of disadvantages with which to deal. If her education prepared her for a job, she cannot assume that she will be prepared ten years later. Skills and fresh enthusiasm fade over time if not put to use. Furthermore, women who have poured their energies into domestic vocations have gained skill and experience, but once they move into the labor market they are once again frightened beginners.

Although many women have employment experience before they begin a domestic career, the employment is often temporary and not taken seriously. Of the many college graduates who look into jobs for which they are overqualified, it is most often the males who are cautioned that the job may not be challenging enough for them, and that it lacks a future. Then the position can be neatly filled by a female, because it is precisely employment without a future for which she is looking. She wants an easy exit to be a continual option. In this way she protects herself from ever having to relinquish work that has become personally important to her.

These attitudes will not do, however, for the woman who goes back to work at age forty and is looking for a new vocation. If work is to be a shot in the arm for her, she needs to become immersed; a tentative and half-hearted attitude will not yield job satisfaction. Although immersion is difficult initially, the woman who is committed to facing each obstacle will find the investment worthwhile, and—in the long run—rewarding.

Making Room for Work. The lifestyle of a housewife is tied to a role that she does not relinquish if she becomes employed. Getting a job is definitely not a move from no work to work. Employed women must trim back domestic tasks to make room for their new vocations, and family members must make adjustments as well.

Unlike men, women who change vocations feel guilty if their new-found work in any way inconveniences their families. For husbands and fathers families sell homes, move across continents, and change schools; such "inconveniences" are accepted as necessary for men's careers and will be tolerated. But for a wife and mother, work is still in the category of luxury and privilege. Consequent inconveniences are not so easily tolerated, because her career is not considered necessary. If her family should be so generous as to make room for her work, she is expected to consider it a gift and relish it as a form of indulgence.

The respect a family shows for its wife-mother's work outside of the home is probably equal to that which they showed for her vocation in the home. If she has taught them to think of her as a worker, the transition will be smooth; if, however, she has let them think of her merely as a convenience, the transition will be rough.

Overcoming Inhibiting Social Prejudice. In the last decade the work field has opened sufficiently that now nearly any woman who wishes can find employment. It is unfortunate, however, that social attitudes do not keep step with legislation and employment policies. Consequently, the greatest remaining obstacles for working women are not legal but attitudinal. Certainly, they may work, but they must do so against society's deeply ingrained view that if a woman is "too successful" she will lose her femininity.

George F. Gilder tries to argue against women working in his book *Sexual Suicide*. When many women are employed, he believes, male pride is bruised and culture decays. Men, because of their sexual instincts, are impulsive, aggressive, and self-interested, but women tame men in order to preserve "the most primary and inviolable of human ties, the one between mother and child."[11] For the sake of their offspring, he argues, women offer sexual privileges to men in exchange for material provisions, protection, and a stable community. According to Gilder:

> A man's socialization—his productivity and his sense of community —will be shaped, perhaps for a lifetime, by the nature of his job and sexual opportunities and pressures during this stage. The outcome is set by work and women. If he finds work that affirms his manhood and a girl who demands that his sexuality be submitted to hers— submitted to love and family—he is likely to become a valuable and constructive citizen.[12]

The implication of Gilder's statement is that men must have the working world because women have the home. Furthermore, his argument centers on a peculiar anxiety. He suggests, in effect, that women ought not to be employed because men have weak egos and that male self-esteem may not survive intact if their last support, employment, is threatened. This is a modern argument. It can only come out of a setting in which men are insecure about work, an economy in which there is widespread unemployment, a technological society in which efficient machines replace inefficient workers, and a society in which money is the measure of a man's worth. If men are afraid that eventually they may not be needed, they share the same anxieties that plague many women in domestic careers. The solutions that Gilder and others like him offer only serve to aggravate the problem. Instead of locking people into roles and blocking out alternatives, we ought to be teaching people to diversify their lives and thereby make their roles more flexible. Encouraging women to take the challenge of employment is one way of helping them move toward new forms of immersion and a broader, richer lifestyle.

6

Emergence

"Home free!"

Sooner of later, even the most involving relationship becomes routine. I have been told by some women that after a decade or so of marriage, they feel as if they had been born married—they can hardly remember when life was different. This settled stage is called emergence. In the relationship between parent and child, emergence occurs as children grow up. As children begin to go out on their own, the patterns of the relationship necessarily change. Emergence is not, however, a casual process that occurs automatically; it often takes hard work. But hard work is one step toward maturity, a difficult but essential part of healthy human relationships. It is unfortunate, then, that such emergence gets scanty, if any, preparation or encouragement.

Emergence does not mean that we outgrow relationships or discard them. Discarding relationships is a waste of human resources; it causes hurt and regret and leaves a trail of emotional scars; it is failure, and not progress. Emergence, on the other hand, conserves our attachments to and investments in others. It is particularly important in the familiar relationships a woman has with her parents, her children, and her husband.

Emergence Between Parents and Children

Emergence between parents and children requires that each make a life separate from the other, with love and mutual respect. This is not as easy as it may at first seem. In childhood there are

83

times when it is difficult for children to distinguish themselves from their parents. Children share their parents' status, security, ambitions, and values, and are encouraged to think that it is for their sakes that their parents accumulate the "good things in life." Because their influence is so strong, few parents are exempt from concerning themselves with how their behavior and character traits affect their children.

During adolescence daughters handle this slippery line of implications—"what my parents are is what I am"—in one of two ways. Either they continue to idealize their parents, or they become hypersensitive to any perceived flaws. Only when children become convinced that they do not have to be what their parents are can they allow their parents to be human. This project of recognizing that parents are neither demi-gods nor total failures marks the transition to emergence.

People in the transition to emergence can be picky about details. For example, Linda hated her father for chewing toothpicks. When she saw him reading the newspaper with a toothpick in his mouth, she could hardly restrain herself from screaming, and accused her father of acting like a "dumb hayseed." Superficially, her complaint seems silly. But emotionally, her reasons were more complex: "Chewing a toothpick is acting like a hayseed, and I am his daughter, so I must be a hayseed too. I don't want to be one, and he has no right to make me into one with his silly habits." Parents and children play this game back and forth, using the appeal, "What will people think of me if you . . . ?" Emergence involves recognition and acceptance of the fact that what parents do is not a reflection on their children any more than what children do is a reflection on their parents. In emergence, this reflecting ceases because the parties are separate. With the separation, the threat that each party formerly posed to the other is removed.

Balancing Communication Between Parent and Child

Before emergence can take place, communications must be brought into balance. In nearly every relationship of parent and child there is an imbalance either of too many negative or too many positive messages. It is helpful as a form of self-assessment for you to ask yourself if it is easier to express criticism and anger or approval and affection in your relationship to your parents. People who more easily express approval and affection cannot imagine themselves voicing disappointments or anger. They are afraid of causing hurt, and even more—of turning loose the powerful emotions that this sort of communication calls for. At the other extreme, some people can be forthright with disapproval, but they become very embarrassed by any direct expression of approval or affection. They excuse their reticence by saying that they do not want to sound mushy, or that their family is not demonstrative.

The words that remain unsaid between parent and child have a way of blocking emergence. A solid, emerged relationship implies the freedom of both to express the negative and the positive. The positive acknowledges what it is that holds the relationship together, while the negative makes differences clear and keeps each person distinct. Affection without the ability for anger and disapproval is not sufficient, because it carries the danger of blurring the boundary between each person. Anger without affection is also dangerous because without the positive, the negative is not worth enduring. The transition to emergence requires filling out the neglected side of communication so that both the solidity of the relationship and the distinctiveness of the persons involved becomes clear.

Learning to Tolerate Distance

Young children spend more time with their parents than adult children do. For this reason adult children and their parents need to learn how they can concentrate communication. The best, though not the easiest way of doing this is through talk. Making the transition from talking to parents as a child to talking to parents as one adult to another takes some concerted effort. The old roles of dependent child and responsible parent easily crop up unless attention is given to overcoming these patterns. Fortunately, certain practical moves can make the transition easier. For example, it is helpful if parent and child find time to be alone so that the presence of others does not magnify old expectations about how parent and child should relate to each other. Meeting on the child's territory can also reduce the effect of parental authority.

Seldom does a daughter have an equally close relationship to both of her parents. In fact, one parent often mediates the relationship for the other. For example, the daughter may carry on serious conversations only with her mother, who then decides how much of it to repeat to the father. Emergence may require a break with that pattern, and getting together with that more distant parent so that both daughter and parent can do their own talking.

These moves toward defining communication between a daughter and her parents make distance tolerable. Giving up the almost daily contacts of childhood presents no problems if communication is meaningful when child and parents are together. The most painful kind of distance in a relationship, however, occurs when they find that whatever time they do have together is empty or awkward. This is not likely to occur in healthy emergence.

Using Symbolic Actions to Promote Emergence

The two most obvious sources of parental power are (1) the financial dependence of their children, and (2) that the children live in the parents' home. Emergence can be signalled and actually helped along by changing these two arrangements from a childlike status to a more adult agreement.

Cutting the financial tie to parents is a significant declaration of independence for a child and for parents. For example, it might mean that the child who was once given money with no obligation is now given a loan. An even more thorough push toward emergence occurs when a child becomes self-supporting. Because money symbolizes power, negotiating the change in a financial arrangement may result in some conflict. One way to reduce the conflict, and maybe even resolve it, is to work toward an understanding of emergence on the part of both parent and child.

"As long as you live under my roof you do things my way" is not only the attutide of authoritarian parents but, to some extent, of all parents. Thus one way for children to emerge is to get their own roofs. Children who move out of their parents' home while immersion is still in process can create a great deal of stress by the same action, but a well-timed symbolic gesture promotes the maturity of the relationship.

Making Expectations Clear

Some of the risk is taken out of emergence if both parent and child can ask of the other what they want out of the relationship. Since it is easy for parents and children to make assumptions about each other that are completely off the mark, double-checking is a good idea. Julia, for example, maintained the tradition of making dinner for her children and grandchildren on their birthdays. As she got older, preparing for these birthdays became quite a project, but she felt she should continue the tradition to please her children. The children, however, occasionally discussed new ways of celebrating birthdays, but always concluded that the tradition should remain to please grandmother. Each was making incorrect assumptions and unnecessary concessions. They were finally able to have an honest discussion about the matter and set things straight, to the relief of everyone involved. Although birthday dinners are hardly monumental, it is easy to see how this pattern of making assumptions could create problems if allowed to confuse more serious matters. Open discussions iron out misunderstandings and pave the way for emergence.

The Price You Pay If You Do Not Emerge

Parents and children who shy away from the work of emergence find that their relationship becomes burdensome, and they find themselves spending energy to keep peace without gaining much in terms of pleasure. Children who do not finish up important issues with their parents end up trying to finish that same business with someone else. This pattern can be seen in many women who have become involved in the women's liberation movement. They are angry at their own parents for pushing them to be hyper-feminine. Out of reaction to them, they do not tolerate any hint of the female stereotype in their daughters. On the other hand women who never emerged from their own parents have trouble letting their own children grow up and emerge.

Children who fail to emerge lose touch with their personal history. Once they are honest with their parents, however, they begin to see how their parents' life saga recapitulates their own. Thus in the very stage in which children achieve the greatest independence from their parents, they also feel a new closeness to them. Children begin to know and accept their parents as they are, and parents learn to accept their children in the same way. Children mellow with their parents' wisdom and parents thrive on children's vitality. Finally, both come to know what they sought to know all along: that given human limits, each cared for the other as much as possible. Relieved, they realize that is as much as anyone could ask.

Emergence in Marriage

When partners know what to expect from each other, and when the pattern of work, shared responsibilities, money, and child-rearing is established, the marriage needs to emerge. Security, contentment, and familiarity take over, and partners become more distant from each other than they were in the stage of immersion. Although neither partner is disloyal, marriage seems less all-consuming. They can feel satisfaction for each other even when that satisfaction is found in an area of the other's life that they do not have in common. In this way, emergence is a time of realism, acceptance, and restfulness.

In the earlier stages of immersion there is a ring of disappointment in the statement "Marriage isn't everything." But the same statement spoken in emergence has a contented tone that implies the acceptance that marriage is good even if it is not everything one would wish for in life. Wholesome emergence allows partners to move beyond themselves and their relationships to find meaning and significance within larger parameters. Psychologist Carl Rogers says about his own marriage of forty-seven years:

> There have been periods of greater remoteness from each other, and periods of great closeness. There have been periods of real stress, squabbles, annoyance and suffering—though we are not the kind who fight—and periods of enormous love and supportiveness. And we always continue to share. Neither has become so involved in his own life and activity that he has no time for the other.[1]

It is clear that Rogers considers his own marriage a good one. He cites as its most significant attribute that both he and his wife were always concerned for the growth of the other. Furthermore, Rogers seems convincd that their individual maturing made it possible for them to grow in their relationship.[2] When he describes how their relationship began, the earliest stage is one of immersion. During his student years, his wife took some courses he was taking. She was an artist, and he, in turn, tried to involve himself in her artwork. In addition, they spent a great deal of time together discussing ideas, interests, and feelings.[3]

Later, Rogers says of this stage: "Consequently, each of us has always had a *separate* life and interest, as well as our life together."[4] It took time and experience for their interests to become separate. He tried painting, but eventually gave it up because when he produced good work it made his wife feel just a little insecure about her own work. When she showed too much skill giving counsel to someone else, Rogers sometimes feared that she would be better than he at his profession. To reduce these rivalries, they had to develop separate interests in addition to their life together.

As they approach fifty years together, Rogers fondly observes that they have shared so much of "suffering and struggle and joy" that they almost know each other's thoughts. "In the middle of some event or scene Helen may say to me, 'Do you remember when we . . . ?' and I say, 'Of course,' and we both laugh together because we know we are both thinking of the same experience."[5]

Rogers seems to cherish each stage of his marriage. The relationship he describes after forty-seven years is one of contented acceptance, in what we might call a wholesome stage of emergence.

Even in a less than wholesome marriage, the stage of emergence results in stability. Energies which at earlier stages were directed toward remodeling the relationship, are redirected toward maintaining a comfortable status quo—even if that involves role-playing and forms of merciful deception.

Virginia Woolf captures such a state of relating in *To the Lighthouse*. Mrs. Ramsey, one of the book's main characters, knows her husband in all his imperfection, yet she does not try to remake him. Instead she acts out of her own hidden strength and lives with his weaknesses as if they do not exist. Both Mrs. Ramsey and her husband sense the deception, but it has become a way of life and a token of their devotion rather than a source of friction.

Perhaps at first glance this manner of accomodating the needs of a partner seems a pretense for a barren relationship. But such a judgment fails to take into consideration the context and history of the relationship and the people who make it up. The Ramseys are not strangers deceiving each other; they have lived a good chunk of their lives together. They know quite well what can and cannot be. Their willingness to pretend is, in a sense, an act of commitment and an indication of maturity. The accomodations they make for each other are not marked by bitter resignation, but by tender acceptance. Only seasoned benevolence can allow them to live with the shortcomings of their relationship in an almost frictionless way. For them, the stage of emergence is marked not by complacency but by acceptance and rest.

Although the problems faced in beginning a marriage and adjusting to the patterns of a shared life are discussed frequently, attention is seldom given to the problems faced later on when married people need emergence. Many women cannot face a marriage that moves toward the stage of emergence, because they assume that keeping marriage alive is the duty of women, and maintaining the stage of immersion is the measure of how well the mission is accomplished. As long as the relationship is intense, women are taught, it is alive. Who can recall an article in a men's magazine giving advice on how to rejuvenate a marriage? I know of none. Yet women's magazines are full of this advice and women read it eagerly, hoping to improve or revive their marriages.

When the methods for prolonging immersion do not work, many women try to fill in for their own lack of an adventuresome life by feeding themselves fiction of one sort or another. Millions of hours are spent watching soap operas and poring over sentimental gothic novels or women's magazines. Absorption in such fiction provides vicarious immersion. Their own lives are dull, the luster of romance has worn off, and the realization breaks through that no future event promises the ecstatic moments of which they dream. These women panic because they do not dare to emerge. Eventually they close their eyes to reality and nestle tightly in their make-believe world. So nestled, they cannot grow.

The marriage that moves into a wholesome stage of emergence is characterized neither by continuous attempts to maintain the intensity of the earlier stages nor by movement into a permanent state of estrangement. Marriage in emergence is characterized by flexible proximity. That is, partners can be together and happy; but they can also be apart without jealousy, insecurity, or loneliness. The movement from closeness to more distance to closeness again is without strain if the skills of communication have been established and trust in each other has been thoroughly tested.

How to Promote Emergence

Emergence does not happen automatically. In fact, very often emergence cannot occur unless women take control of their relationships and make it happen. Because instinctively we may want to hold off emergence, we need to consider the benefits of this stage, which allows for a large payoff of comfort for a relatively small investment of energy. Carl Rogers' description of his own marriage exemplifies this: he and his wife know each other so well that they can communicate with unfinished sentences and simple reminders of events from the past. As long as a relationship is kept up to date, as was theirs, its familiarity creates great efficiency and comfort.

Diane, a middle aged woman, once told me that her newly married daughter had critically questioned her about how she and the girl's father could tolerate separation so easily. The father's work required that he travel, and sometimes he was gone for several weeks at a time. During her husband's absence, Diane—who had interests of her own—became particularly involved in her vocation. While her father was gone, the daughter asked her mother if she was lonely, and Diane replied in all honesty that she was not.

Pressed by her daughter to judge if her marriage was still healthy, Diane concluded that it was. Her confidence stemmed from knowing that she and her husband kept each other informed of their own activities, they each knew the other was happily engaged in something fulfilling, and that they had learned how, after an absence, to spend some concentrated time together to prevent a lasting distance from coming between them. The time they spent together was not out of duty. They wanted and needed this time in order to stay familiar with each other. Their relationship, although not continuously intense, was an important source of comfort and security for both of them.

Security is another advantage of relationships in emergence. Relationships in this stage offer a comfortable background for new ventures. It is a very good feeling to know that you may risk yourself in one domain without putting your entire source of well-being on the line. In fact, the self-confidence often found in persons who have lived through relationships to the emergence stage seems to transfer to new situations and relationships. Perhaps the old principle of not having all your eggs in one basket is in operation, giving these people the courage to take on new challenges.

In spite of the benefits, some people are afraid of emergence. Why? Although emergence is itself a comfortable state for a relationship, the transition from immersion to emergence can be difficult. Before being able to move into emergence, it is necessary to finish up what remains to be done in the immersion stage, those things which have been put to one side because they are awkward, painful, or upsetting. For example, college students who are moving into an emergent stage with their parents often bring to a close the expectation that they will live at home when they are not at school.

Bringing this stage to a close requires some intricate communication at the risk of each party misinterpreting the other. The parent who suggests independence may be interpreted as withdrawing support and writing off the child; on the other hand, the child who seeks this independence may leave parents with the impression that ties are being broken because of ill feeling. Emergence can only work smoothly if both child and parent are able to recognize that they are moving into a new but desirable stage in their relationship.

Working out the status of the relationship in the emergent stage may very well require a transitional phase of high energy investment as the immersion stage tapers off. In fact, before emergence is possible, marriages often go through a stage of crisis. During this crisis phase hours of talk, arguing, bargaining, planning, or even seeing a counselor may be necessary. Nevertheless, instead of drawing the relationship back into immersion, this intensity smooths the way for a new style of independence and distinctiveness. What appears to be a breakdown of the marital relationship is, in fact, only partners outgrowing their immersion-stage style of relating. If a new pattern of attachment can be found, the marriage revives; if emergence is too long overdue, however, the marriage may disintegrate completely.

Emergence, like the other stages of a relationship, can be controlled. Unfortunately, this stage is not given much public recognition: there are few good models for it and little available advice. Therefore emergence takes special ingenuity. If you take your relationship seriously and are determined to mature, you must be willing to put your creativity to the test and learn the skills of emergence.

7

Charting Your Course

"I know where I'm going
and I know who's going with me . . ."

—*American Folk Song*

There is a peculiar mentality that says distress is a virtue, and for many Americans having a crisis has become a status symbol. In the past few years numerous articles have satirized the woman who sees that everyone else is having a crisis and doesn't want to be left out. This attitude deserves the knife of humor. Any woman who takes herself seriously will do some thoughtful life-planning in order to avoid unnecessary emotional pain.

If you are going to take charge of your life, you will need to know how to maintain a healthy balance in your relationships and ventures. The first step is to become sensitive to the stages of development within relationships. By taking care to be thorough about your predispositions, and by having the endurance to see relationships through to emergence, most of life's crises can be averted.

Recognizing Problems of Imbalance

The healthiest life pattern is one that has several predispositions in the process of formation, enough immersion to make the present vital, and enough emergence in long-term relationships to lend stability. Three patterns of imbalance signal problems: too little predisposition, too much immersion, and too litle emergence.

93

Knowing the danger signs for these stages and some strategies for avoiding them is useful for life planning.

Too Little Predisposition: "I don't know what to do."

If you ask yourself what you might be doing ten years from now and you find that you cannot even imagine what you might *like* to be doing, you are probably having trouble forming predispositions. If you wait too long, you may find that old interests have settled into a routine and nothing new is opening up. The result is depression, a lack of enthusiasm, and a bleak vision of an empty future. Your inability to enjoy life may produce a negative attitude toward other people's happiness—people with empty futures seem to begrudge others a vigorous interest in new ventures.

Women without predispositions often not only feel empty, they act empty. Lacking luster, they seem unable to carry on interesting conversations and would rather be entertained than entertain. Such women will often communicate by discussing problems; but in contrast to women who ask for genuine help and support, these women refuse to solve their problems. Why? Because solving problems inevitably leads to getting on with the business of life. Women without predispositions—without business to get on with—would rather cling to their old problems than find new solutions.

Earlier in this book we discussed ways in which false expectations can limit our growth. Women with too little predisposition are especially victimized by these misconceptions—"My sister was always so good at that, I guess I'm not smart enough to . . ." But once we rid ourselves of the mistaken notion that we are victims of our childhoods, we see that though we are adults, our lives do not have to be rigidly set. Therefore, it is never too late to take charge of planning our lives. Unless we live deliberately, we will remain emotionally childish regardless of our chronological age. It is important to remember that life neither begins nor ends at age twenty. Adulthood also has stages, and each one has something new to offer. If we simply wait for changes to force themselves on us, the transitions are difficult and the results unsatisfactory. But if we become responsible and develop foresight, these changes can unfold richly.

Finding a remedy for lack of predispositions takes time.

However, recognizing that need is the first step. Once you have identified the problem, you will need some time to begin forming prospects for the future. Often just knowing why it is necessary to go through the predisposition stage helps relieve the restlessness. Later on in this chapter we will discuss some active steps you can take to encourage your predispositions to grow.

Too Much Immersion: "I don't have a moment to spare!"

Too much immersion is just what it sounds like—treading water in a sea of endless tasks. All that swimming takes energy. If you are immersed in too many things at once, you are sure to become exhausted and confused, and your life will become hectic and joyless. When high investment has focus, however, it is possible to put out enormous amounts of energy and actually thrive on the heavy demands. In fact, you actually get back in enthusiasm the same amount of energy you put out as work. But if emotional investment goes in too many directions at once, feelings of fragmentation result and the satisfaction of immersion is lost.

One sign of over-immersion is the loss of spontaneity and imagination in relationships. A woman who has too much to do has no reservoir of energy to use for being original, adventuresome, or creative. Consequently, she becomes preoccupied with how things are *supposed* to be; she meets the demand but does not enjoy the challenge. Another sign of over-immersion is the language a woman uses to talk about relationships. When immersions turn into heavy obligations, the language of duty is heard more frequently: "All marriage should . . ." "Aren't good mothers supposed to . . ." "If I'm going to be a good daughter I'm going to have to . . ."

Taking the pressure off of immersion depends on straightening out your priorities instead of trying to deal with all of your immersion relationships at once. This can be done by asking yourself certain questions: Can any of these commitments be moved forward into emergence? Could any of these commitments be dealt with more effectively at a later time? Of these commitments, which ones require immediate attention?

A parent's relationship to an adult child is a good example of an immersion stage that can be moved forward to emergence by some deliberate efforts. One way for a mother to encourage her child's emergence is to stop treating her son or daughter as a little child; at the same time, she must request that her child not treat her as a parent. This means that the parent and child treat each other with the same consideration and respect for boundaries that friends practice. Of course, they cannot and should not break the parent-child bond, but they can redefine it by practicing a new style of being together.

In order for a parent and child to practice new patterns in their relationship they have to spend time together and avoid situations in which others push them back into their old habits. One mother I know meets her college-age son in a restaurant for lunch. These occasional lunches give them a chance to be alone together, away from their familiar home turf. Moreover, neither has the passive role of guest, because they have chosen a place both can afford and they each pay their own bill. This arrangement has been so pleasant that they have agreed to do it whenever vacation time makes it possible. Besides having fun, it is a way of making a strong symbolic statement about how they want their relationship to be.

Sometimes what appears to be a problem of too much immersion is in fact a problem of too much interference with immersion. This problem especially affects the working mother. United States labor statistics report that more than fifty percent of married women are now employed outside the home. A significant number of these women have small children. Immersion in employment and immersion with children, it appears, can be carried on together quite successfully; but special efforts must be made to keep more immediate and incidental demands from interfering with these two important commitments. Women in this position learn to say "no" to unimportant ways of being busy. Housekeeping becomes less important, trivial socializing is avoided, and certain blocks of time are set aside for children and work during which interruptions are not tolerated. A woman who makes deliberate efforts to control her own life patterns and conserve her own energies finds sufficient time to work, be with children, and do other things that are important to her.

Too Little Emergence: "It's just not the same as it was . . ."

Problems of emergence result from lack of endurance. Some persons can endure the adventure of immersion, but cannot persist afterwards in maintaining the relationship. This lack of emergence has its most telling sign in desertion and repetition.

People, for example, who divorce and remarry because the blush of romance is past, believe that they could keep romance blushing forever if they could just find the right partner. This same pattern can be found in people who desert their parents to avoid complications, or in friends who drift apart and then are awkward and disinterested in each other when they meet again.

In *Scenes from a Marriage*, Ingmar Bergman skillfully captures what can happen to a couple when emergence is blocked. Frustrated because neither of them has found the perfect marriage, Peter and Katerina become attached to each other out of disappointment and hate. Loosened up by a little liquor and wallowing in self-pity after some cruel verbal combat with his wife, Peter says:

> I wonder whether there is anything more horrible than a husband and wife who hate each other? What do you think? Perhaps child abuse is worse. But then Katerina and I *are* two children . . . Right inside Katerina a little girl's sitting and crying because she has fallen and hurt herself and no one has come to comfort her. And I'm sitting in a corner and haven't grown up, and am crying because Katerina can't love me even though I'm nasty to her.[1]

Peter and Katerina have an agenda. It is pathetic and cruel because it is their retaliation for disappointment and unfulfilled hopes. Their agenda is also intense. They are close, but like a body to its own diseases. Each is a mirror for the other's weaknesses and they seem unable to get far enough outside of themselves to reorient, to give the other a chance, or to refocus on the good of the other. Because they are unable to accept the limitation of their marriage, they are unable to emerge. Ruthlessly, they magnify each other's failures until finally they discard each other in divorce. This is a childish but all too familiar way of dealing with blocked emergence.

One healthy strategy for dealing with blocked emergence is to seek the help of a mediator. The mediator need not have magical powers in order to be effective. Perhaps his or her mere presence is most important, as it signifies the couple's commitment to work on their problems. Considering how difficult the transition from immersion to emergence can be, however, a mediator can also be a significant source of advice. Getting a counselor's help, for example, can be an efficient way of accomplishing work that might otherwise take much longer.

A second method of promoting emergence is to begin with some partial emergence in one problem area. Money, because it represents power, is often an area of contention in marriage. Since emergence involves some separating of power after the close partnership of immersion, a couple that squabbles about money might try to establish an emergence agreement for handling finances. Perhaps they can divide the income and give each control of half, or switch the bookkeeping responsibilities from one partner to the other. Whatever the strategy, if it reduces conflict and creates some boundaries between partners, it helps to introduce them to the pattern of emergence.

Assessing Your Life

To begin life planning, you must know where your life stands right now. Then you will be able to decide in what directions you would like to move in the future, and what steps you can take to set the process in motion. To give you some idea of the process of life assessment, we'll use Jane's life as an example.

Jane's Life Plan

Jane is thirty-eight years old, and she has been married to George for twenty years. They have an eighteen-year-old daughter, Vickie; a sixteen-year-old son, Bill; and a thirteen-year-old daughter, Tracy. Jane has worked at various jobs off and on throughout her marriage, but always part-time and never at a job she really liked. Her parents live about five hundred miles away, but they visit once a year and the whole family visits Jane's parents during vacations. She and George socialize a great deal, but she doesn't have close friends of her own. She hasn't given much thought to the future, but when pressed for an answer she says that she hopes her kids turn out well, that her parents won't be troubled with the problems of old age, and that her family will stay healthy and happy. Sometimes she thinks about getting a job, but she doesn't know what she would want to do.

On Chart I, Janes's life looks like this:

Chart I: Where do I stand?

Themes	Predisposition	Immersion	Emergence
Husband		X	
Children:			
Vickie		X	
Bill		X	
Tracy		X	
Parents		X	
Vocation:			
Homemaker		X	
Employment	X		
Friends	X		
Other			

With the chart filled in, Jane is able to take a closer look at each theme and decide how she feels about it. She must give special attention to four questions: (1) What makes this theme or relationship important to me? (2) What makes it important to others? (3) What kind of time do I spend on it? (4) How much satisfaction do I get from it?

What is Jane's Relationship to Her Husband? "We love each other, we have three children, and we've been together for twenty years. That's a long time! When we are together, we usually go out to a party or invite people to our home. My husband has two golfing buddies, and we often get together with their families after the guys finish their game. We're home together sometimes, but then we watch T.V. or work around the house. Sometimes I worry that we're not as close as we used to be. We don't talk things over very much. I don't think that's the way it should be, but I don't know what to do about it."

Although Jane and her husband have continued the habits of immersion in some things, they no longer spend time with each other unless other people or distractions are present. That is probably why they do not talk: they are either too busy or too distracted. Although their relationship is ripe for emergence, it will not happen until they change their communication habits.

What is Jane's Relationship to Her Children? "They're my kids—that's why they're important to me. Kids are always important to their parents. I suppose I'm important to them because I take care of them. I think mothers ought to give their kids self-confidence and the security that everything's okay. My older daughter has a job after school and in the summer, so she's away quite a lot. My son is a nice kid, but sometimes he has a big mouth, and that worries me a little. I don't have any trouble with my youngest. She's still sort of my baby, even though she's thirteen."

Jane's children still need her, but not as much as they used to for daily care. Her oldest daughter is becoming independent, and Jane is a little uneasy about the growing distance between them. Her son's rebellion worries her because she is afraid she will lose control of him. Finally, the fact that her youngest child is still her baby seems to give her some reassurance.

The time Jane spends with each of her children tends to be time she spends with them all; her attention is not focused on each personally. Although the immersion stage with her youngest daughter will probably last for several more years, her oldest daughter is ready for emergence, and her son will soon follow. If Jane is going to maintain a wholesome relationship with these two older children, she will have to move into emergence with them.

What is Jane's Relationship to Her Parents? "I owe them a lot. They made sacrifices for me when I was growing up. Now their children are all they have, and I think it's only right for us not to disappoint them. They're proud of me. I've got two brothers; one is divorced and the other doesn't have too much to do with our family. My parents think I'm a model daughter with a model family. I know they brag about us to other people. We get along pretty well, but some little things irritate me. I don't like it when they call me "dear Janie," and I don't like it when they criticize me for spoiling my kids. When they feel bad about saying something, they turn around and make it up to me by giving us some money or presents or something."

Jane is still quite dependent on her parents. Sometimes their visits together are tense times during which she feels burdened down with the duties of being a daughter. Moreover, she admits that her decisions are based on what her parents would think. Although she would like to gain some independence, she feels guilty about separating from them. Her guilt is related to the fact that she feels she owes her parents a repayment for their care of her in the past. Unfortunately, none of this has ever been openly discussed because she never visits her parents without her husband or children. Of all Jane's relationships, this one needs emergence most urgently.

How Does Jane Feel About Her Vocation as Homemaker, and the Possibility of Working Outside the Home? "I guess I would call myself a 'bored housewife.' I used to be a perfectionist housekeeper, but lately I've been slacking off a bit. I'd like to get a job or something. Working with people sounds good to me. I've got this friend who works for a travel agent, and sometimes she tells me about the fantastic trips she plans for people. I actually feel jealous of her, and it gets me down a little because I'd like to be doing what she's doing. I don't know if my husband and kids could take it, though. They're used to having me at home to hold the fort."

These comments give the impression that Jane is vocationless. She does not get much satisfaction out of being a homemaker, but she feels obligated to meet the needs of her husband and children in this way. Apparently, she has not given serious thought to a vocation; all she does is look on with envy at the work of her friend. Even in this she does not give much credit to her dreams.

How Does Jane Feel About Her Relationship to Her Friends? "Most of the women I know are the wives of George's friends. We get along all right, but we're not really close. The only thing we really have in common is our husbands. I'd like to know Betty, the woman who works for the travel agent, a little better. But sometimes I think she must look down on me because I'm just a housewife. It would be nice to have someone to really talk to besides my husband."

Jane's comments about her friends show that she is still immersed with her husband, as most of them are the wives of his friends. She would like to have friends of her own, but feels a little awkward. However, it would be an important step for her to begin developing outside relationships.

Where Does Jane Stand, and What Should Be Her Goals? Jane is over-immersed. The complexly interwoven set of relationships with her husband, children, and parents have tied her down. With no significant interests outside the family, she must face the fact that her family is slowly outgrowing her. The family relationships she describes seem fraught with obligation and deficient of pleasure. If she could alter some of these relationships, Jane would probably enjoy them more and be happier in general.

Reasonable goals for Jane would be: (1) To begin to emerge into a more satisfactory relationship with her husband. (2) To begin letting go of her two older children. (3) To stop feeling like she has to be her parents' ''dear Janie'' and achieve a more adult relationship with them. (4) To begin to break away from her outworn role of homemaker and start to think about what kind of work she would like to do. (5) Try to make some close friends of her own, whom she doesn't necessarily have to share with George. On Chart II, Jane's goals look like this:

Chart II: Where do I want to go?

Theme	Predisposition	Immersion	Emergence
Husband			X
Children:			
Vickie			X
Bill			X
Tracy		X	
Parents			X
Vocation:			
Homemaker			X
Employment		X	
Friends		X	
Other	X		

What Steps Must Jane Take to Accomplish Her Goals? Jane's first step is going to be a visit to her parents, by herself, for a four-day weekend. During that visit she is going to talk to them about herself, and about her relationship to them. She will try to get up enough courage to ask them—or if necessary tell them—to get ready for some changes. She will have to make it clear to them that the debt is as paid as it ever will be, and that she is no longer going to define her relationship to them in terms of obligations. Once she makes this clear, she will be ready to explore what kind of friends she and her parents can be. She must also be ready to deal with her parents' possible hurt, anger, or bewilderment without backing down from her position. One four-day weekend may not be enough, but it will be a good start.

Jane's second step will focus on her relationship to her husband. She recalls that when they were first married they always went out either Friday or Saturday evening for dinner. That was their time together, and they rarely invited anyone else to join them. Once they had children, they gave up this pleasant routine, but Jane is going to ask that it be reinstated. It will be understood that the children will not be included in this time together.

For her third step, Jane is going to arrange a vacation with her oldest daughter, Vickie. They both like movies and theater, and Jane is going to see if she can arrange a modest theater trip to New York through her friend who works for the travel agent. Jane is particularly excited about this plan, because she thinks she and Vickie will have a good time together. They will have time to talk and get reacquainted, the chance for a vacation like they never had before.

Jane is still dreaming about getting a job, but needs some time to keep dreaming while she works on getting some of her important relationships into the emergence stage. Part of her predisposition for getting a job will involve preparing her husband, children, and parents for the fact that in the future their "dear Janie" may be changing. Visiting her parents alone, going on a vacation with her daughter, and spending more concentrated time with her husband are already good clues to her family that she plans to take some deliberate action in her life.

Finally, Jane realizes that although she has been very close to her parents, she has been distant from her brothers. In fact, the break was so complete that she did not originally include them on her chart. After entering her brothers on Chart I as predispositions, she enters them on Chart II as immersions. She realizes that she herself has helped her parents to make comparisons between "Janie and the boys" that were both unfair to her brothers and unhealthy for herself. In view of this, she is determined to renew contact with her brothers by writing them some letters and even seeing them, if that proves possible.

She also intends to take some positive action about making new friends. She can start by asking Betty to lunch downtown, near the travel agency. Although she knows it will take time, Jane is hopeful that she and Betty can enjoy each other's company in a different way than she has done with the wives of George's friends. While she is still busy thinking over the possibility of employment, Betty can serve as a mentor for Jane because she had to face the same sorts of decisions when she decided to look for work outside the home.

The kind of self-assessment that Jane has carried out, and the rather specific plans that she has made for herself are her attempt at life planning. What she is doing is not magic, it is work. Just making each decision will not be enough; she will have to stick by each and see it through. More self-assessment will have to follow as Jane begins to see some relationships change. She may decide after carrying out a few steps of her plan that it needs some modification. She will probably meet with some resistance from family members who don't want to see her change, and she will need determination tempered with understanding to make them see why the changes are necessary.

Your Life Plan

Now you can begin to untangle those threads we talked about at the beginning of the book. Your first task will be to separate and identify each one. Only then will you be able to see where it came from, where it seems to be going, and how it can be woven into the overall pattern of your life.

To begin filling out Chart I, find a quiet spot where you won't be disturbed for at least an hour. Then ask yourself the following questions:

What Are the Major Themes in My Life? Try to find a one-word abbreviation for each of the major themes in your life. These may be the same as Jane's—husband, children, parents, friends, vocation—or you may have some of your own, such as school, bicycling, gardening, cooking, painting, sister, and so on. When you have decided what the themes are, list them in the first column, "Themes."

Where Do I Stand in Relationships to Each Theme? Think about how you feel about each of your themes. What is your relationship to each? Is it something you would like to be more involved in (predisposition); something you are currently involved in (immersion); or something that is stable and established (emergence)? If you feel conflict or excitement about the theme, it is probably in predisposition or immersion. If you feel comfortable with it, it is probably already emerged. After each theme, mark the appropriate column with a check, to indicate where you stand right now. For example,

Sample Chart I: Where do I stand?   Today's date_____

Theme	Predisposition	Immersion	Emergence
1.			
2.			

Now begin filling in your own chart on the next page.

Getting to Know Yourself

If you had no trouble filling in Chart I, congratulations! You seem to know yourself pretty well, and you are probably ready to move on to the next step, setting your goals. However, if you had difficulty figuring out how you felt about each theme, or even coming up with themes, you probably need to get to know yourself better.

To get the most out of relationships, you must know what it is you really want—not what others expect you to want or what you think you should want. In order to do this, it is necessary to know yourself. This may seem relatively easy, or even absurd, in view of the fact that you've lived with yourself all your life. But for many women, it can be a difficult and frightening journey—so frightening that some women never embark at all.

Who Am I? To talk truly about yourself—not just the socialized outer layer you present to the world—often seems beyond possibility. Women in particular often remain silent almost instinctively if they have been taught to believe that what is feminine is weak and inferior. Because of this uncertainty, communication about the self at the deepest levels of identity often takes the form

Chart I: Where do I stand?   Today's date_____

Theme	Predisposition	Immersion	Emergence
1.			
2.			
3.			
4.			
5.			
6.			
7.			
8.			
9.			
10.			

of confession—"I'm not really a very good mother . . ." "I should call my folks more often . . ." and so on.

Why is it so hard to be honest with ourselves? Because admitting what we really want, need, and feel often means changing habits of years' standing, admitting we may have been wrong about certain things, and embarking on hard and perhaps painful work. Real change cannot take place, however, until we can be honest with ourselves. Deep down inside we know what we need, and we will not let ourselves be satisfied until we get it. The more rocks we pile in front of the door to our desires, the harder those rocks will come tumbling down as, someday, they must. It is much healthier to lead those desires out into daylight, confront them, and begin work on them than it is to hide them, feed them, and let them grow until they become unrecognizable monsters that demand to be let out.

Each of us lives with a certain friction between who we are and who we feel we ought to be. For example, who wants to admit to being weak when she is expected to be strong, or even strong when she is expected to be weak? It is frightening to feel atypical, and this fright strangles communication. Yet open communication is the best way to resolve doubts and free the self for growth. Communication occurs most easily when there is an assumption of confidence, acceptance, and protection.

The journey into the interior, the search within the self, can be carried out individually and in solitude. It is, however, considerably enriched when it is shared with others. Through the process of communication, experiences are focused, meaning is enriched, and the fear of finding a self that does not fit this world is reduced. A big discovery is made: everyone has problems, not just you!

For a woman who is already engaged in efforts to be aware and reflective, there is often a lingering anxiety that accepting the invitation to explore the interior of the psyche will leave her in a closed-off, locked-in, and isolated world. But the inner world and the outer world are not so discontinuous. For when we close off portions of our inner world, keep our deepest psyche quarantined from others, we must also close off areas of our outer world. What we cannot acknowledge in ourselves we cannot accept in others. Consequently, when our indifference to ourselves is taken full circle, it becomes indifference to others.

When Anaïs Nin speaks of publishing her journals, she insists that bringing herself out of hiding was a form of fulfillment and hope and a bridge to others. Still, the vehicle was her journal, her private or inner world, the fruits of her introspection. She says of sharing her journals:

It was not without misgivings because all of us are afraid to be mis-
understood, not to be loved, to be condemned in fact for what you
expose. What happened is that I suddenly found I was having an in-
depth communication with others which is really . . . one of the
dreams of our life . . . I suddenly found, you see, that it was only by
communicating very deeply in terms of emotion, in being able to
tell others what our dreams are, without making fun of them, some
of them could be fulfilled.[2]

The Different Me's I Am. When you begin trying to isolate
your "self," you will immediately see that it is unclear where the
self begins and where it ends. The self seems to overflow into
everything, changing from moment to moment and dashing away
capriciously just as we think we have captured it. It is tempting to
try to define yourself as if you are a distinct, an irreducible entity:
this and nothing else is my self. One reason this is tempting is
because it also seems to give us a way to define the outer-
world—our situation. But when we attempt to define "self" and
"outer-world" as if one quantity were X and the other non-X, we
find that our concepts correspond very poorly, if at all, to the way
we actually experience "self" and "world." No matter which term
we define first, meaning is lost when we take one away from the
other. The "self" is always a self in a particular situation; and the
"situation" is always influencing the self.

We cannot, however, do away with these concepts. Even
though they escape us when we try to analyze them, in our or-
dinary, common-sense experience we are able to discriminate between them. In our everyday sense of experienced self and experienced world, we do not rigidly isolate one from the other, nor
do we confuse them. In day-to-day experience, self and world are
somehow held together as two terms in an irreducible unit. We
sense the meaning of "self," and at the same time sense that it
flows "into everything that belongs to us—and then flows back
again."[3]

It is precisely because our sense of identity comes out of the
dynamic interaction between ourselves and our world, and
because that environment is many-sided, that we too become
many-sided. As a result, our "self" becomes composed of many
potential selves, some of which may even seem to be opposites:
the ability to be leader or follower, passive or active, strong or
weak, adult or child, dependent or dependable, feminine or

masculine, analytical or creative, all according to what the moment calls for.

When a woman looks in the mirror at her own image and says to it, "My goodness, I don't know who you are," she is caught in the bind of trying to locate herself in isolation from the many arenas in which the many sides of her person are expressed. Furthermore, she is confused because she does not know where to stop the action, what moment in time to choose as the one in which she is really herself in her truest form. Looking in the mirror she is doomed to find very little. How then should she proceed?

We can never really get to know ourselves if we persist in believing that the self must remain consistant through time, must be forever and always the same. Everyone realizes, says the wise, Christian psychiatrist, Paul Tournier, "that the ideal of personal fulfillment requires continual leaping forward, and that one can not leap forward without letting go of something behind."[4]

Growth, process, and change are not capricious. As the various sides of the character expand, as the arenas of experience open up, there is a pattern of progression. Understanding the pattern of progression enhances self-understanding. Blocking change for the sake of consistency only results in rigidifying the self and impoverishing experience, not in clarifying identity or making it stronger.

Some Practical Exercises for Making Your Own Acquaintance

Once you get over the fear of meeting yourself on a dark street, remaking your own acquaintance can be an exciting experience. One reason you may have forgotten some important things about yourself is that, in trying to please others, you tried to become what you thought they wanted you to be. But no one is completely molded by the environment, and once upon a time you may have known more about yourself than you do now.

1. Try to Remember. Try to remember back to a happier time. This may be last year, last month, or back to your early childhood. Why were you so happy? Were there particular things you did then that you don't do now? Nancy was depressed because she didn't seem to be interested in anything any more. She even stopped meeting new people because she thought of herself as such a boring person. When she tried to remember her happiest time, it was when she was five or six years old. She used to draw pictures, write little stories, and read herself to sleep every night. She was surprised to realize that in trying for so many years to be "grown up," she had dropped all of these pleasurable activities out of her life. She was so tired each day that at night she fell right to sleep, and the same exhaustion robbed her of the enthusiasm for creativity she used to possess. An easy way for Nancy to begin getting to know some new things about herself was simply to allow time for her reading, special time just for herself. This in turn helped her to remember other things she liked to do, and eventually she was able to explore those areas as an adult and to make rich additions to her life. An added bonus was that in "remembering" some old things about herself, she was also able to "remember" what she wanted to do, and began naturally to develop new predispositions and immersions.

2. What You Read About or Dream About Can Tell You Who You Are. Do you like to read books about pioneer women? See movies or television programs about Victorian England? Read romantic thrillers? Do you ever wish you could write for a newspaper, drive a truck, or be a doctor? Pay attention to the sorts of things you think are good entertainment, they might tell you things about yourself you hadn't realized. For example, if you admire pioneer women you might try giving expression to the woman in you who is an adventurer, who likes to try new things, or be surrounded by nature.

What you fantasize about is a good clue to the sides of your personality that may need more expression. Don't be afraid to dream, and don't be afraid to take your dreams seriously.

3. Ask Someone Who Knows You. Your self-conception may be—and probably is—radically different from the person others think you are. If you really want to know who you are, find out how you appear to other people. They may not give you a version of yourself that you agree with, but you will certainly be surprised how many different versions of yourself are out there walking around.

Ask enough different people so that you are sure to get a variety of responses, then look at those responses. Do any of them ring true? Is there any particular version to which you can say, "Yes, that's me, that's just how I am"? Why do you think others don't see you in the same way you see yourself? Once you begin to get some idea who you are, or who you might be, you'll find yourself making decisions that are more and more in conjunction with your true intentions.

Some Practical Exercises for Developing New Predispositions

Getting to know yourself can help you see clearly where your life stands, and it's the number one exercise for developing new predispositions. Here are some others.

1. Write a Letter. It may help you to sort things out if you can put them down on paper. Not everyone is a good writer, but everyone has written letters. Try writing a letter to yourself. Tell yourself what you've been doing lately how you feel about it, and so on. If you're stuck, say so. For example, you might begin like this: "Dear Me, I don't even know why I'm writing you because I can't think of a thing to say. Not much has happened since the last time I wrote, I'm still doing the same old thing—staying home and watching the kids, doing the housework, and wishing life was more exciting. I sure don't want to do this for the rest of my life. You know what I'd really like to do? Someday I'd like to be able to . . ." This may seem like a very silly thing to do, and it is. But it's so silly that it may help you free yourself from your usual ways of thinking and actually help you get your thoughts in order.

2. Talk to a Friend. Some people feel more comfortable talking than writing. Talking to a trusted friend can help you get your feelings out so you can see them in perspective. The friend, remember, is not there to give you advice; he or she is just there to listen—to act as a sounding board. As such, your friend can allow you to hear your own words, what you're really saying. For example, you might say, "Ruth, sometimes I feel so down I don't know what to do, and other days I wonder what I was so upset about. Is it going to be like this for the rest of my life? Nobody told me that when you got married and had kids, your life had to stop, but that's sure what it feels like . . ." Don't worry about whether your feelings are positive or negative—they're your feelings and that's where you have to start, although it certainly isn't where you want to end.

3. Find a Mentor. Find another woman who has already been through what you're going through. Ask her what she did when she was in your position. Compose a list of questions to ask her, such as: When you were going through this, did you feel like it would never end? What finally happened to break things up? Did anyone help you, or did you have to do it yourself?

Mentors can also be found in books, and autobiographies are an especially good source. They are generally written later in life, when the person has emerged from most of the relationships that were in immersion earlier. Such books can offer good advice, and can help us to remember that everybody has problems, even the most successful. Some of the books I have used for mentors in writing this book are the diaries of Anaïs Nin, *Becoming Partners* by Carl Rogers, and *Scenes From a Marriage*, which draws on real life to make its point. You will find your own, based on your own needs and interests. Also by reading a book you may see what you do not want to be; you may discover some helpful negative images.

4. Create Diversions. Take the pressure off—let's face it, you're probably not going to come up with a fresh predisposition tomorrow. In fact, one reason why you are having such trouble coming up with new predispositions may be because you are trying too hard. Decide that you're not going to think up any predispositions for six months or a year. In that time, begin to do new things. You can begin by shaking up your schedule, breaking your routine. If you have a poached egg for breakfast every day, have scrambled eggs one day instead. If you usually clean the house from nine to twelve, take a walk at nine and clean from ten until one. Breaking up your routine is an excellent way to remind yourself of something you've probably forgotten: things don't have to be the way they are, and you have the power to change them.

Once you've begun to change your routines, schedule new activities to fill up old time slots. Continue your walks, take a class, have lunch with a friend, grow a garden, ride a bicycle, read a book—anything you like, just make sure you don't expand your old activities to take up all your time.

Most of all, enjoy yourself. Don't eye every new thing you do in the hope that it may turn out to be a predisposition. If you relax and give yourself some room, all the while being attentive, you may find that predispositions will begin to take shape.

5. Consult a Professional Counselor. Sometimes our problems seem so burdensome that we just can't solve them ourselves. If this is you, it's a positive step to accept the fact that you need help getting started. Talk to a professional, someone whose business it is to deal with problems—this may be a social worker, psychologist, or your pastor. Don't worry about boring them or shocking them, they've heard a lot of different stories and are there to help you with yours.

Once you've given yourself a chance to remake your acquaintance, and taken the pressure off yourself to come up with all of the answers, give Chart I another try.

Chart I: Where do I Stand?   Today's date_____

Themes	Predisposition	Immersion	Emergence
1.			
2.			
3.			
4.			
5.			
6.			
7.			
8.			
9.			
10.			

Setting Your Goals

Now that you know where you stand, where would you like to go? In trying to design a life plan, it is helpful to ask yourself, "What will my life be like when I'm thirty, forty, fifty, and so on?" A twenty-year-old woman asking this question must realize that there is no choice she can make at twenty that will fill up the next fifty years of her life. In fact, it's not likely that any choice she makes at age twenty will fill up even the next fifteen years of her life.

In filling out Chart II, think about how you'd like your life to be in the next ten years. Don't think ahead to how you're going to achieve these goals, and don't worry beyond the ten-year timespan. Remember that no decision you make now is irrevocable.

List Each of Your Themes, just as you did on Chart I. Think about your life ten years from now. What do you think the important themes will be then? If there are some new themes, add them to your list.

Now Think About Each Theme Individually. In what stage do you hope these themes will be in ten years? Ask yourself the same questions Jane asked: (1) What makes this theme special to me? (2) What makes it important to others? (3) What kind of time do I spend on it? (4) How much satisfaction do I get from it? Mark the appropriate column for each theme, just as you did in Chart I.

Sample Chart II: Where do I want to be in ten years?

Theme	Predisposition	Immersion	Emergence
1. Mom			X
2. Husband		X	

Chart II:
Where do I want to be in ten years?   Today's date_____

Theme	Predisposition	Immersion	Emergence
1.			
2.			
3.			
4.			
5.			
6.			
7.			
8.			
9.			
10.			

Practical Exercises for Determining Your Goals

If you know exactly where you want to be in ten years, congratulations again! You're probably ready to proceed to the next step, achieving your goals. But if you had a hard time deciding where you'd like to be in ten years, try to discover what is preventing you from gazing into the future.

1. Change the Time Span. Ten years may be too long a time for you to think about. Each woman has her own perception of the amount of time she needs to make a change. Try changing your goal to five years, or three years, or one year, or six months. On the other hand, if ten years is still too near, try twelve years or fifteen years. Whatever it takes to get you to look ahead and determine your needs is the right amount of time.

2. Talk to a Friend. Choose a friend you trust, and who can act as a sounding board—he or she must be able to listen *without* giving advice. All you want to do is talk out the problem. Sometimes when we do this, the answer pops out all by itself. For instance, if you've been jealous of your sister for years because she was always considered "the pretty one," and you don't know where you want to go with the relationship, try talking it out.

"You know," you might begin, "I haven't gotten along with my sister for years. I realize now that it's because Joanie was always prettier—or at least I always thought she was prettier—and I've always held it against her. I suppose it's not her fault, but I still don't know what to do about it. It's been so many years that maybe we could never be friends. On the other hand, I've never had the nerve to talk to her about it. Hey, maybe I'll call her up and see how she feels. If she doesn't care, well, we've never been close anyway. But I guess it's worth a try . . ."

3. Write a Letter. If it's easier for you to write your feelings down, write a letter to the person involved. You can actually mail it, or read it aloud, or just use it as a sounding board for your feelings. The main thing is to get your thoughts out. For example, "Dear Joanie, I bet you're surprised to hear from me! I've been thinking about that. I mean about why we're not close, like sisters are supposed to be. One thing is that I guess I've always been jealous of your looks. I never thought I could be as pretty as you are. Now that we're adults, though, it seems sort of silly to go on thinking like that, and letting it come between us. I'd really like to talk about it with you . . ."

4. Talk to a Professional. If you can't see the forest for the trees, a professional counselor may be able to help you get to the root of your problems. You don't have to do everything yourself!

Ready to try it again? When you think you've gotten a better handle on what you'd like to do, fill out Chart II again.

Chart II:
Where would I like to be in _____ years?   Today's date_____

Theme	Predisposition	Immersion	Emergence
1.			
2.			
3.			
4.			
5.			
6.			
7.			
8.			
9.			
10.			

The Means to the Goal: How Am I Going to Get There?

You've done a lot of work. You've sorted your threads, perhaps untangled a few knots, and it should be clearer to you where you are and where you're going. Only one question remains: How are you going to get there?

Compare Your Self-Assessment Now (Chart I) with your self-assessment ten years from now (Chart II). What themes have changed?

On Chart III, List each theme, your goal for that theme, and your means for achieving that goal in the proper columns. State your means briefly, but be specific. Broad generalizations do not help.

After You've Listed the themes, goals, and means, look at your list again and decide in what order you should begin working on your themes. For example, you may have immersion in school at the top of your list, but in order to accomplish that you will first have to emerge the relationship with your daughter. So in the ''Order'' column you would list your daughter as 1 and school as 2.

Sample Chart III:
How am I going to get there?   Today's date_____

Theme	Goal-stage
1. School	Immersion
2. Parents	Emergence
3. Daughter	Emergence

Practical Exercises for Achieving Your Goals

Deciding on the specific means to your goals takes a lot of thought. You're not just dreaming now, you're getting ready to turn your dreams into practical reality. They may have been your dreams at the beginning, but what you do with them is bound to affect those close to you. Make sure that you have allowed space for the important relationships in your life before you plunge ahead into new immersions.

If you had difficulty working out how you plan to achieve your goals, give the following suggestions some thought.

1. Everything Comes in Its Own Time. You don't have to accomplish your goal tomorrow at noon—that's why you set yourself a ten-year goal. You are free to reach your goal at any time within your limit, and to use as much time as it takes to get there. For example, if going back to school is a predisposition now and an emergence ten years from now, your plan might go like this: I'll give myself a year to explore my interests and decide on the field I want to study. Then I'll send away for as many school's catalogs as I think fit my interests and finances, and study the information.

Means	Order
Send for catalogs from different schools, see which ones look interesting—visit schools I'm interested in—apply—enroll.	2
Have dinner with mom and dad, tell them how I feel about our relationship, see what they think. Work toward treating each other as adults—see them each individually, like I would do with my friends.	3
Get her ready to assume more responsibility by teaching her some of my jobs—have her make some dinners, let her have some afternoons when I'm not home so she can learn to handle the house, make sure she understands why I want to go back to school.	1

Chart III:
How am I going to get there?   Today's date_____

Theme	Goal-stage
1.	
2.	
3.	
4.	
5.	
6.	
7.	
8.	
9.	
10.	

Means	Order

Then I'll make arrangements to visit the schools that look interesting and see what they really have to offer and how I feel about them. I'll apply to the ones I really like, and when I'm accepted I'll enroll and begin my immersion.

2. Think About Your Present Commitments. When you are newly inspired with fresh predispositions, the tendency is to rush right out and experience them. But before you can put your ideas into action, you must be sure that you have made room for them in your life. This means that you must prepare those people who may be displaced by your new activities.

For example, you want to put your predisposition for employment into immersion by taking a full-time job, but your children have been accustomed to having you home in the afternoon when they return from school. Here's how you might set your goals: First I'll talk to the kids about why I'm going back to work and make sure they understand what kinds of changes it will mean for both of us. We'll spend a few weeks or months practicing what it will be like for them to come home when I'm not here. They can learn to do some of the things I usually do—get dinner started, pick up a few things at the store, take full responsibility for cleaning up after themselves, walk the dog. Maybe they can get interested in after-school activities one or two days a week. When we all feel confident, I'll start looking for a job.

3. Get Your Priorities Straight. You may know where you are and where you'd like to be, but the road ahead may be strewn with obstacles. This is especially true for the woman who is presently over-immersed. If this is you, try to figure out why. Is it because you are still doing things for others that they could do just as well themselves? Few of us like to admit that we're not indispensable, but let's face it—at least some of what we do can be done just as well by someone else. In fact, by doing so many things you may be depriving others of the satisfaction of doing things for themselves. Call your family together and tell them frankly what the problem is. "You know, I really need more time to myself to work on my art, but I'm so busy washing and cleaning and driving you kids places that I don't have a moment to myself. Tom, I've been picking up after you for a long time. It was okay when you were just a kid, but you're old enough now to take responsibility for your own things. It would save me a lot of time—and I'd be a much easier Mom to live with—if you would start doing that one thing for me. Jenny, you're starting junior high next month. I think you're old enough now to start taking the bus to your gymnastics class by yourself, don't you? After all, you're going to have to start sometime . . .''

4. Living Through Your Immersions. That road to your goal may be strewn with obstacles that you have no control over. If you are a new mother, for example, you will probably be immersed in your child for a few years. Don't waste the opportunity. Enjoy this immersion as much as you can before you begin trying to bring it to emergence. It's important to try to live each moment as fully as possible, keeping in mind that nothing lasts forever. Someday you may even look back on those days of diaper-changing with nostalgia . . . Living in the future and ignoring the present is not only frustrating, it robs us of the pleasures of the present.

Have any of your ideas changed concerning how to reach your goals? If they have, try completing Chart III again.

Chart III:
How am I going to get there?   Today's date_____

Theme	Goal-stage
1.	
2.	
3.	
4.	
5.	
6.	
7.	
8.	
9.	
10.	

Means	Order

One Last Word . . .

Does all of this planning mean that you've turned self-centered and self-indulgent? No, it doesn't. Planning your life includes being thoughtful of others and responsible toward them. Just drifting along is far more likely to result in thoughtlessness toward others. Planning your life is also a way of acknowledging that God made you a person with many possibilities for healthy emotions, wholesome relationships, and joyful adventures. Discovering and living out those possibilities is a way of saying "thank you" for the gift.

Does planning your life mean you are not leaving it to the Lord anymore? Actually it means just the opposite. When you do your very best to find a responsible life plan you are trusting that God will show you a way to be everything He has intended for you.

If you actually want to put your life plans in context go stand under an open sky and say:

Thank you God for giving me a life to live.

I'll do my best with Your help;

I won't lose courage because I know You're faithful.

If you trust that God is faithful, you have reason enough to go ahead and plan your life the best you can.

Notes

Preface
1. Becker, Ernest. *The Denial of Death* (New York: The Free Press, 1973), pp. 257-258. This quotation is Becker's paraphrase of Kierkegaard's "knight of faith" image.
2. Bonhoeffer, Dietrich. *Letters and Papers from Prison* (New York: The Macmillan Company, 1967), pp. 150-151.

Chapter One
1. "Sixteen Going on Seventeen." From *The Sound of Music*, RCA Victor, LSOD-2005.

Chapter Two
1. Freidan, Betty. *The Feminine Mystique* (New York: Dell, 1963), p. 68.

Chapter Three
1. Fromm, Erich. *The Art of Loving* (New York: Harper & Row Publishers, 1956), p. 39.
2. Friday, Nancy. *My Mother, Myself* (New York: Delacorte Press, 1977). This book details the love-hate relationship that exists between mothers and daughters.
3. de Beauvoir, Simone. *Memoirs of a Dutiful Daughter* (Baltimore: Penguin Books, 1963), p. 39.
4. Boston Women's Health Collective. *Our Bodies, Our Selves* (New York: Simon and Schuster, 1971), p. 5.

Chapter Four
1. Bergman, Ingmar. *Scenes From a Marriage* (New York: Bantam Books, 1974), p. 126.
2. de Beauvoir, Simone. *The Second Sex* (New York: Bantam Books, 1961), p. 495.
3. Rollin, Betty. "Motherhood: Who Needs It?" *Women's Liberation*, Michael Adelstein and Jean Pival, eds. (New York: St. Martin Press, 1972), p. 67.
4. *Ibid.*, p. 68.

Chapter Five
1. Smedes, Louis B. *Sex for Christians* (Grand Rapids: William B. Eerdmans Publishing Co., 1976), p. 179.
2. Morgan, Marabel. *The Total Woman* (Old Tappan: Fleming H. Revell Company, 1973), p. 71.
3. May, Rollo. *Power and Innocence* (New York: W.W. Norton and Company, Inc., 1972), pp. 117-118.

4. Deutsch, Helene. *The Psychology of Women* (New York: Bantam Books, 1973), p. 346.
5. Fromm, Erich. *The Art of Loving* (New York: Harper & Row Publishers, 1956), p. 40.
6. Weingarten, Violet. *A Woman of Feeling* (New York: Alfred A. Knopf, 1972), p. 219.
7. *Ibid.*, p. 219.
8. *The Bible*, Ecclesiasticus 6:14-17.
9. Rossi, Alice. "Sisterhood is Beautiful," in *Psychology Today* (August 1972), p. 40.
10. Woolf, Virginia. *A Room of One's Own* (Baltimore: Penguin Books, 1945), p. 97.
11. Gilder, George. *Sexual Suicide* (New York: Bantam Books, 1975), p. 258.
12. *Ibid.*, p. 101.

Chapter Six

1. Rogers, Carl. *Becoming Partners* (New York: Delacorte, 1972), p. 24.
2. *Ibid.*, pp. 28-29.
3. *Ibid.*, pp. 22-23.
4. *Ibid.*, pp. 27-28.
5. *Ibid.*, p. 29.

Chapter Seven

1. Bergman, Ingmar. *Scenes From a Marriage* (New York: Bantam Books, 1974), p. 23.
2. Nin, Anaïs. From a public lecture, May 1974, Calvin College, Grand Rapids, Michigan.
3. James, Henry. *Portrait of a Lady* (New York: Signet, 1903), p. 186.
4. Tournier, Paul. *A Place for You* (New York: Harper & Row Publishers, 1966), p. 184.